MW01490884

Zacharias Tanee Fomum

# DAILY DYNAMIC ENCOUNTER WITH GOD

Éditions du Livre Chrétien
4, rue du Révérend Père Cloarec
92400 Courbevoie France
editionlivrechretien@gmail.com

FIRST EDITION, 1988, 10 000 COPIES.
THIS BOOK HAS ALREADY BEEN PRODUCED IN 76 000 COPIES.

SITH EDITION, 2002, 3 000 COPIES.

Printed by :

**Editions du livre chrétien**

4, rue du Révérand Père Cloarec

92400 Courbevoie - FRANCE

Tél : (33) 9 52 29 27 72

Email : editionlivrechretien@gmail.com


Covert by :

Jacques Maré

# Table of contents

# PREFACE

This book, "DAILY DYNAMIC ENCOUNTERS WITH GOD," is one of the books in the series, "Practical Helps for Overcomers". The books in this series which have already been written are:

In this book, the possibilities are offered through Bible meditation, prayer and obedience, for the overcomer to enter into a daily encounter with God that will transform every aspect of his walk with Him. God can indeed be heard and met everyday, and many times a day. He is waiting to be heard. He is anxious to talk to His children, to hear them and to answer them. He is not silent. You can encounter Him today and He can encounter you, and you will never be the same.

We send this book out with prayer that it might be used by the Lord to bless and deepen the walk of His children with Him, and thereby accomplish the purpose of God for man, which is that he should know Him, live in Him and enjoy Him for ever!

Yaounde, 7th June 1987

Zacharias Tanee Fomum
B.P. 6090  Yaounde
Cameroon

# CHAPTER 1

# THE LORD JESUS AND DAILY DYNAMIC ENCOUNTERS WITH GOD

"*And in the morning, a great while before day, he rose and went out to a lonely place, and there he prayed*" (Mark 1:35).

"*I thank thee, Father, Lord of heaven and earth, that thou hast hidden these things from the wise and understanding and revealed them to babes*" (Matthew 11:25).

"*Father, I thank thee that thou hast heard me. I knew that thou hearest me always*" (John 11:41-42).

"*I glorified thee on earth, having accomplished the work which thou gavest me to do; and now, Father, glorify thou me in thy own presence with the glory which I had with thee before the world was made*" (John 17:4-5).

"*That evening, at sundown, they brought to him all who were sick or possessed with demons. And the whole city was gathered together about the door. And he healed many who were sick with various diseases and cast out many demons; and he would not permit the demons to speak, because they knew him. And in the morning, a great while before day, he rose and went out to a lonely place, and there he prayed. And Simon and those who were with him pursued him, and they found him and said to him, 'Every one is searching for you.' And he said to them, 'Let us go to the next towns, that I may preach there also; for that is why I came out.' And he went throughout all Galilee, preaching in their synagogues and casting out demons*" (Mark 1:32-39).

## LIFE'S GOAL

For a life to succeed before God, it must be goal-oriented. If your goal is nothing, you will accomplish it; that is, you will accomplish nothing! Purposelessness is a disaster. The number one reason why most people fail in life is that they do not have a clearly defined goal for their lives. Because there is no clear goal, they have no clearly worked out method or plan to accomplish their goal and they are, therefore, not able to work out the discipline that is necessary for them to accomplish the goal.

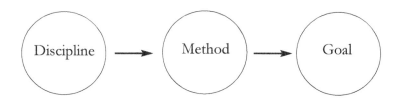

The goal must determine the method that is to be used and impose the discipline that is necessary for it to be accomplished. Goals are indispensable.

A man's accomplishments cannot be separated from his goals. A person's goals make him into what he ultimately becomes. Below are some characteristics of goals.

1. Goals must be clear.

2. Goals must be specific.

3. Goals must be measurable.

4. Goals must have a time limit for their completion.

5. Methods must be evaluated and the best ones chosen for the accomplishment of the desired goal.

6. Goals demand a man's all in order to be accomplished. If a man holds back anything from his goal, he has also decided not to accomplish it. This is the choice between discipline and indiscipline.

7. Those who make the most success have only one overriding goal.

8. Goals must be large or big enough so as to engulf all small desires. They must be such that when accomplished, they will leave an impact on history.

9. The goal of the believer must be so big that nothing short of divine intervention and the putting in of his all, can save him from failure. They must be big enough to legitimately demand a person's everything.

The Lord Jesus had a goal. It was clear. He accomplished His goal before He went back to heaven. He put it as follows, "*I glorified thee on earth, having accomplished the work which thou gavest me to do*" (John 17:4). The goal of Christ was to glorify the Father on earth. He glorified the Father by accomplishing (finishing) the work that the Father gave Him to do. He had said earlier, "*My food is to do the will of him who sent me, and to accomplish his work*" (John 4:34). Anything that was truly the Father's will contributed clearly to the one task of accomplishing His work. His work and the Father's will were inseparable. If He did the Father's will every second of His life, He would accomplish His goal, for His goal was accomplished by doing that Father's will every second. Each action then was a part of the whole.

A man may plan to build a fifty-storey building. He must conceive the whole house and draw it out. He must "see" the completed thing in detail and then he must set out to work at it. In order that the building should become what it was meant to be, each portion of the building must be correct. The foundation, wall, roof ... must each be correct. Every brick must be laid correctly. We can take the laying of each block as the second by second activity of a man's life. If each individual block is well-laid, then the building will become what it was meant to be. Individual blocks that are poorly laid, spell disaster for the whole project. No one can say that he is just placing one of one million blocks, and that that one can be wrong provided the rest are correct. A correct structure demands the correctness of every issue. Brethren, this is most challenging. It means that in order that I may accomplish the goal of God for my life, I must be right with God every second of my life. It means that I must be where He wants me to be every second of my life. I must be doing what He wants me to be doing at that second, and I must be doing it the way He wants me to be doing it and for the reason for which He wants me to be doing it. Any time when I am in the wrong place or doing the wrong thing, or doing the right thing the wrong way, or doing the right thing at the right time, in the right way, with the wrong motives, I stand in God's way.

So, to succeed, the overall plan of the house must be drawn and the finished house seen. Then every detail in the building must be carried out according to the specifications of the architect.

God is the Master-Architect. He has His overall goal for our lives. We must receive that goal from Him and then we must work hard God's way and accomplish it. We must be in the right place every second and we must be doing the right thing. We must compromise nothing; for compromise will contribute to the collapse of the building one day. It is possible to put the wrong materials and plaster them so that no one knows that they are the wrong materials. It may even look very good. However, when the storm shall come, that which is hidden and false will not only be exposed, it will lead to the collapse of the whole house. All the secret sins and faults that are not dealt with radically may remain hidden for a life-time, but at the Judgment Seat of Christ, where all shall be tested and exposed, those who have built with such materials will see their beautiful, massive structures collapse and they shall go away unrewarded.

God works according to a master plan. He planned world salvation from the foundations of the world. He mapped out everything with precise dates. In the fullness of time, He sent the Saviour, Jesus Christ. In the fullness of time, He will send Jesus a second time, not to save but to reward His own. He has His Kingdom in view. He is working at that Kingdom. He is moving towards it. All events are ordered to lead to it. He will succeed.

Your life must be goal-oriented. You must "see" what you must do. You must put all of yourself into it and be sure that all goes God's way. The goal of Jesus was to do the Father's will and accomplish His work. He, however, accomplished this goal by doing specific things. He preached the gospel. He healed the sick. He delivered the possessed. He trained the disciples. He had a specific programme. He did not make everyone into a specific disciple. He had the seventy-two, then the twelve and even among the twelve, there were the three whom He prepared in a more intimate way. He did not stay in one place until all the sick who could be brought to Him from all that region had been brought to Him. He healed all who were brought to Him at particular times and then moved on to new places. He worked hard at accomplishing His goal. He said that accomplishing His goal was His meat.

## LIFE'S PRIORITIES

As we have seen, the Lord Jesus had a goal and He gave Himself to it. It is obvious that at each instant there were many things that He could do. There were :

> very bad things,
> bad things,
> neutral things,
> good things,
> very good things,
> best things,
> all opened to Him.

It is needless to say that the very bad things, the bad and the neutral things were all forbidden to Him by His very nature. But what of the good, better or best things? What was He to do? What did He do? If there was a choice between ministering to an individual and ministering to a crowd, what did He do? If there was a choice between healing the sick in one place and moving to another place to preach there also, what did He do? How was He guided?

Jesus was not guided by a desire to impress multitudes. He was not guided by a desire to reach billions. He was not moved by a desire to perform the most spectacular miracles. He was guided by the Father's will, and the Father's will imposed certain priorities on Him.

The priorities of the Lord Jesus were the "musts" of His life. He gave Himself to the "musts" of His life. When faced with many things, He chose to do that which, according to the Father, was a must for Him at that moment. He said the following were "musts" for Him.

1. "*And he said to them, 'How is it that you sought me? Did you not know that I must be in my Father's house?'* " (Luke 2:49).

2. "*And when it was day, he departed and went into a lonely place. And the people sought him and came to him, and would have kept him from leaving them but he said to them, 'I must preach the good news of the kingdom of God to the other cities also, for I was sent for this purpose'* " (Luke 4:42-43).

3. "*The Son of man must suffer many things, and be rejected by the elders and chief priests and scribes, and be killed, and on the third day be raised*" (Luke 9:22).

4. "*Go and tell that fox, 'Behold, I cast out demons and perform cures today and tomorrow, and the third day I finish my course. Nevertheless, I must go on my way today and tomorrow and the day following; for it cannot be that a prophet should perish away from Jerusalem*" (Luke 13:32-33).

5. "*Zacchaeus, make haste and come down; for I must stay at your house today*" (Luke 19:5).

6. "*And I have other sheep, that are not of this fold, I must bring them also, and they will heed my voice. So there shall be one flock, one shepherd*" (John 10:16).

Each of these "musts" were indispensable for the accomplishment of His overall purpose.

By a daily commitment to the "musts" of His life, Jesus accomplished His goal. He refused to do good, better or the best things. He did the things that were "musts". The "musts" varied, but they were each indispensable for the goal to be accomplished God's way and in God's time.

## THE PRIORITY OF PRIORITIES
## OF THE LORD JESUS

Not all priorities are the same. There is the priority of priorities. At the tender age of twelve, the Lord Jesus had understood this and expected His parents to understand that His number one task was to be in His Father's house. He was saying that the priority of priorities for Him was to be alone with His Father. He did not only say it. He lived it out. The Bible says: "*And in the morning, a great while before day, he rose and went out to a lonely place, and there he prayed. And Simon and those who were with him pursued him, and they found him and said to Him, 'Everyone is searching for you.' And he said to them, 'Let us go to the next towns, that I may preach there also, for that is why I came out.' And he went throughout all Galilee, preaching in their synagogues and casting out demons*" (Mark 1:35-39).

The priority of priorities of the Lord Jesus was to have a daily dynamic encounter with His Father every morning.

## TIME FOR THE PRIORITY OF PRIORITIES

The Bible says that Jesus rose up in the morning. We state then that the morning is the time for the priority of priorities. We also read that although it was in the morning, He actually rose a great while before day. He woke up at a time which permitted Him to have plenty of time with His Father before it was day. Why did the Lord Jesus choose the morning as the time for meeting God? The following are some of the reasons:

1.  He decided that He would not see the face of man before He had seen the face of God. He loved His Father supremely. He loved human beings as a manifestation of His love for His Father. He decided that He had to see the face of the One He loved the most before He would see the faces of the people whom He loved as a manifestation of His love for Him.

2.  He decided that He had to talk to God about men before He talked to men about God. He was well aware of the fact that only God could move men to act God's way. Therefore, He chose to let God act on behalf of man before He would tell man to respond to the acts of God. There is so much talking to man about God and too little talking to God about man these days. Is this not the reason why there is so much failure in our day? The cart is being put before the horse and that is why there is no corresponding action to God's glory.

3.  He knew that the early morning hours were the best. His mind was not crowded. His thoughts were fresh and His energy was unused. He could then approach God with all His heart and with all his soul and with all His body. He knew that He grew tired with the activities of the day and

that His strength of concentration and the strength of action diminished as the day wore off. Since His encounter with God was of primary importance, He gave the earliest hours to it.

4.  He knew that the encounter with God was the most important event of His day. He, therefore, gave the best time to the most important event.

5.  He met God in order to receive instructions, guidance and direction for the day. If the instructions He received were to be applied, they had to be received before the time of application. If He did not meet God before the day, He would go into the day with His own ideas and not God's. If He met God in the afternoon or evening, He would have spent a part of the day messing things up. What would have been the use of coming in the evening to receive instructions that ought to have helped Him to walk and to work, during the day, after the heart of God? If a person wants to go to the west and He starts off in the morning and does not check his bearing, but spends the whole day pushing to the east with full force, and at the end of the day, he gets out his map and compass to see how far he has gone, that would be foolish. He ought to have sorted things out in the morning, and by evening he would have found out that he had made progress in the right direction. Knowing this, the Lord Jesus made it a must to meet His Father a great while before day.

6.  He needed power from His Father to accomplish each day's work. He had to receive the power before He went to work. If He went to work without the power of God, He would have gone out to obvious failure.

We see clearly that the most important encounter between Jesus and His Father was in the morning. There were other encounters in the day but the morning encounter was the most important.

The Psalmist also made the morning a time for meeting God daily. The Bible says: "*O Lord, in the morning thou dost hear my voice; in the morning I prepare a sacrifice for thee, and watch*" (Psalm 5:3).

"*But I will sing of thy might, I will sing aloud of thy steadfast love in the morning*" (Psalm 59:16).

"*But I, O Lord, cry to thee, in the morning my prayer comes before thee*" (Psalm 88:13).

From the example of our Lord, we say that each believer should meet God everyday. He should meet God every morning, a great while before day. My personal recommendation is that all disciples should wake up and be ready to meet God at 4.00 in the morning. They should spend the time from 4.00 to 6.00 seeking God and communing with Him. There is no substitute for this.

## A PLACE FOR THE PRIORITY OF PRIORITIES

We are told that the Lord Jesus went out to a lonely place and there He prayed. His place for the priority of priorities was a lonely place. Why did He choose a lonely place? The following are the reasons:

1. He wanted to separate Himself from man so as to be separated unto God. He was constantly in demand by man. Even when

He was tired and resting, there were always needs that made people turn to Him. Had He not sought a lonely place, it would have been impossible for Him to have the time that He needed with His Father without human interruption. As can be seen, even though He withdrew to a lonely place a great while before day, they still sought Him and went to Him. He was, however, able to have His intercourse with His Father because He woke up a great while before day, and because He went to a lonely place where it took time for those who wanted Him to find Him. So He sought a lonely place to avoid being disturbed by those seeking Him.

2. He wanted a lonely place so as not to be disturbed by noise and other distractions. He wanted to concentrate on His Father and, to do so, He put away all distractions by going to a lonely place.

3. He wanted a lonely place so as to give Himself without reservation to His Father. Lovers always want to be alone. They always want to separate themselves from all the others and to concentrate on the one they love. Jesus, therefore, wanted a place where He could give Himself to His Father in an uninhibited way.

4. He sought a lonely place because He did not want to be like the hypocrites who drew the attention of men to their praying. He wanted His Father alone to know the intensity of His longing after Him.

5. He sought a lonely place because He did not want to disturb others with His communion with God. His communion with God involved cries and tears. How could He utter loud cries with tears to God where others were doing other things that did not permit noise? He, therefore, sought a lonely place.

## HOW DID THE LORD PRAY?

The Lord Jesus sought a lonely place and there He prayed. How did He pray? The writer of the Epistle to the Hebrews allows us to catch a glimpse of how He prayed. He says, "*In the days of his flesh, Jesus offered up prayers and supplications, with loud cries and tears, to him who was able to save him from death, and he was heard for his godly fear*" (Hebrews 5:7).

Jesus offered up prayers and supplications. He did not just offer a prayer and a supplication. He offered up many prayers and many supplications. He brought everything before God. He begged God. He prayed aloud. He cried. He wept. He prayed as a desperate person. He was desperate. He did not take for granted that because He was doing the will of God, God was obliged to back Him. God was under no obligation. He did not say that God would have to act in order to save His honour.  God is under no obligation to save His honour.  His honour is guaranteed, regardless of what anyone does and regardless of what happens. The Lord Jesus knew that if He did not pray, God would not act.

God has decided to act in accordance with the co-operation that He receives from His co-workers. Although He can do everything without them, He has decided that if they pay the price, some things will happen; and if they do not pay the price, those things will not happen.

The Lord Jesus, knowing that in each miracle there was God's part, which man cannot do and which God alone must do, and man's part which God will not do if man does not do it, decided that He must do that which He had to do; so that all that God wanted to happen would happen. He, therefore, put all of Himself into it. He prayed and prayed and prayed. He supplicated. He uttered cries and tears. He stormed heaven. He prayed in such a way that God had to answer. He did not only whisper.  He prayed aloud. Then he uttered cries, and at the height of it all, He uttered loud  cries.

He did not only cry. He shed tears. He had to receive answers.

God looks for tears. He pays attention not only to a person's prayer but to his posture in prayer and to the presence or absence of desperation. He wants to be made to feel compelled to act. He said to Hezekiah "*I have heard your prayer, I have seen your tears; behold, I will heal you; on the third day you shall go up to the house of the Lord. And I will add fifteen years to your life. I will deliver you and this city out of the hand of the king of Assyria, and I will defend this city for my own sake and for my servant David's sake*" (2 Kings 20:5-6).

The Lord heard the prayer and saw the tears. Hezekiah provided the Lord with something to hear and something to see. The Lord, on hearing that which was to be heard and seeing that which was to be seen, decided to do the following for the sick king:

1.  Heal him.
2.  Add fifteen years to his life.
3.  Deliver him and the city out of the hand of the king of Assyria.
4.  Defend the city.

What if Hezekiah had only prayed and not wept? What if the Lord had heard the prayer but, on looking, had seen no tears? Probably, He would have done half of what He did or any portion of it. If the king had only prayed, he might have been healed; for that is what he sought. The other three things were bonuses which were reserved for those who paid the extra price.

Could that be the reason why many of God's children do not enter into His full glory? The things that God has, do not automatically become those of His children. The things that God has, and how they may become the lot of the people, can be divided as follows:

10. God's best in totality.

9. May be received by those who pay the total and the supreme price.

8. May be received by those who pay an additional price.

7. May be received by those who have been delivered completely from the love of the world, and so on.

6. May be received by those who pay an additional price like further dying to self, more intense prayer, more fasting ...

5. May be received by those who pay an additional price in the School of obedience, like entering into a higher degree of sanctification.

4. May be received by those believers who pay a price in the School of obedience, like praying, fasting ...

3. May be had by all who have received the new birth, without any asking on their part.

2. May be had by those human beings who, although they do not know Him, live according to the limited light that they have received.

1. May be received by all human beings, regardless of their attitude towards Him.

*What may be received from God depending on the price paid*

The thought that people can receive anything from God regardless of their attitude to Him and their co-operation with Him is foolish. Why does God not just save every human being because Christ has died on the cross? The answer is that He will only save those who repent and believe the Gospel. If the whole world were to repent and believe the Gospel, He would save everyone. If none were to repent and believe the Gospel, He would save none even though the Saviour has died on the cross. Why did He not allow the entire army of 32,000 to go out and fight with Gideon? Why did He disqualify all except the 300? The truth is that He sends to battle only those who are qualified to fight, and they qualify through paying the price of self-denial. Why is His eternal purpose not tied to everyone who says that he has believed? Why is His eternal purpose only tied to the overcomers? The truth is that only the overcomers are true believers. Those who do not overcome never believed. Man might have thought that they believed, but before God they did not.

That the believer must press on in order to have the best from God, is further illustrated in two lessons which the Lord taught. The friend at midnight only got the loaves because he persisted. If he had not persisted in knocking, he would have gone away as he came — empty-handed. The widow only got the judge to do her justice because she wearied him by her constant visits and requests. If she had been less persistent, she would have gone away unsatisfied.

Elisha asked for a double portion of the Holy Spirit that rested on the prophet Elijah. Elijah did not say, "Oh I have a good servant who wants to do great things for God. He has asked for a great thing. He has much faith. Let me give him at once because God gives without price." *He instead said to him, "You have asked a hard thing; yet if you see me as I am being taken from you, it shall be so for you; but if you do not see me, it shall not be so"* (2 Kings 2:10). Elisha was to receive his request if he fulfilled a condition that demanded that he fix his gaze on Elijah and look at nothing else. He did and when Elijah was being taken away, he saw it and cried, "*My father, my fa-*

*ther! the chariots of Israel and its horsemen"* (2 Kings 2:12). Because he paid the price, a double portion of the Holy Spirit that rested on Elijah came on him and he performed twice as many miracles as the senior prophet.

The best of God's gifts are conditional. They are given to those who will, in their exercise of faith, co-operate the most with God. Such people already manifest, by their previous relationship to God, that they mean business with God and are prepared to leave no stone unturned so as to have God's best.

God will not give anyone anything that the person does not want. He will not throw pearls to swine. Those who ask receive. Those who seek find and to those who knock, it is opened. Those who do not ask, do not receive. Those who only ask will not receive that which is received by the one who seeks; and those who seek must seek diligently and with their whole heart. However, there are things that only the violent who wage full war can receive. Knocking says that there are obstacles to be overcome. These obstacles are overcome by those who pay the price.

Jesus prayed. He supplicated. He cried loudly. He wept. That is how He prayed. Those who would see God answer their prayers as God answered His, must:

1. Have the same attitude to prayer that He had.

2. Put their all into prayer as He did.

3. Be as desperate in prayer as He was.

4. Press on (without giving up) as He did.

My dear friend, you are as spiritual as you want to be. If you want to be more spiritual, you can be by paying an additional price. You can enter into God's glory if you want. However, you must want His glory enough to be prepared to pay the full price of removing everything in your life that stands in His way, and putting on all that has to be put on.

## WHY HE SO PRAYED

We have seen that Jesus offered up prayers and supplications with loud cries and tears. Why was He so desperate in prayer? The answer is that He could not have been otherwise. His ministry depended entirely on divine intervention. If the power of God moved, then He would be successful. If the power of the Lord did not move, then He would fail utterly. So He had to have God move. He offered up prayers and supplications with loud cries and tears to the One who could save Him from an impotent ministry.

Can you imagine them bringing all the needy to Jesus and He would speak to a demon to come out of a man and nothing would happen? That He could speak to a leper saying, "Be clean," and the leper would continue to be leprous? That He could command a paralytic to walk and the paralytic would continue to be paralysed? That He could call out to a dead man to be raised and the dead man would continue to be a corpse? If that had happened, He would Himself have been like a corpse; for can a corpse impart life to another corpse?

Since the ministry of Jesus was totally dependent upon the movement of God in might, He knew, therefore, that each day, He had to settle with the Father the fact that He (the Father) would back Him (the Son) with His abundant presence and manifestation of power. He, therefore, came to the Father determined to win in prayer, or fail absolutely. If the Father heard Him, all was well. If the Father did not hear Him, all was ruined. He, therefore, came to His Father every morning, not as a matter of a routine to be performed, but as a matter of life or death. No one needed to remind Him to come to the Father each morning. The ministry before Him made it the one burden of His heart. Until He had met the Father and had settled all that was going to happen with Him, He was restless. The time in the morning when Jesus met the Father was, therefore, the most important time of the day. It was also the most indispensable. He then put all of Himself into it, as a soldier who knows that he must have ammunition before going to the warfront each day.

So, fearing lest He should go out and be unbacked by the Father, He pleaded, He cried and He wept. The Father heard Him and met His need, and this guaranteed success in each situation.

The tragedy of our day is that we are faced with the same situation that Jesus faced. We are confronted with demon-possessed people on the right and on the left. There are captives all around. Some are bound by lust, others by hate, others by greed, others by alcohol, cigarettes, and so on. We are surrounded by multitudes who claim to belong to Christ, but sin rules in their lives. Others who know deliverance from sin are yet bound by the love of self, the love of the world and the like. The sick are all over: the blind, the lame, the maimed, lepers, and people with all kinds of diseases. These are not only around us in the world but they are around us even in the church. There never was a day when so many who confess to be saved are handicapped by one disease or the other. We preach to the whole world by radio, television, books, crusades, and every possible means. We put millions or billions into it, but if we want to be honest, we have to admit that we are not equal to the task. No one seems to be able to produce the quality of life and ministry that the New Testament so readily promises to be that of the normal believer. The average believer or minister is impotent. Most of those who claim to be successful have lamentable failures which they hide. If everything came out into the open, perhaps most, if not all, would fall before God and cry out, "I am dead. My ministry is impotent. My life is full of failure, defeat and greed. I get angry, irritable, touchy, hard and indifferent. My motives are mixed. My heart is divided. I love You, but I love myself even more. Self rules my life, and so on."

Why does this cry not come out? I think the reason is that we have refused to be honest. We are able to go on and deceive many without the manifestation of God's power in our lives. We are deceived and the church prefers to be deceived, and so it goes on. We boast about that which we ought to be most sorry about. We have failed and we boast in our failure. We know too little of God to be bothered. We care too little about the plight of the world to cry out to God in desperation. Unlike Jesus, we are content with an impotent ministry.

Oh! that God would deliver me from this condition of death! Oh! that He would touch my heart and open my eyes to see what a hindrance I am to Him (for an impotent ministry is worse than no ministry). Oh! that He would move in might in such a way that I would leave everything aside - all the things that I am doing for Him in a ministry that lacks the full power of the cross and the Holy Spirit, and, like Jesus, go and ask Him and receive the indispensable power to represent Him, and have the full holiness of God worked out in me - that holiness without which no one shall see the Lord. It is in the direction of seeking the Lord, praying, supplicating with loud cries and tears, fasting and fasting and fasting, that I must direct my life from now henceforth, until the Lord heals my barrenness and backs my ministry with interventions from above. Until then, my ministry lacks mandate. Lord, help me!

Do you see the same need in your life and ministry? Do you see the need to fast, pray, wait before Him, put away all sin and all evil motives ... and continue in that condition until He moves from heaven and brings in a new day? May He grant you to see, and, as you see and withdraw and begin to seek Him, pray also for me who must henceforth give myself to seeking Him and waiting on Him until He answers from above and brings down His glorious power and His all-glorious presence. Pray also for one or two others, that the Lord may lead them in the same direction. Continue to pray until all impotent ministers abandon their impotent ministries and withdraw to seek God. Then the Lord will be exalted and His purpose will be accomplished.

## THE EFFECT OF HIS ENCOUNTER WITH GOD ON HIS DAILY LIFE AND MINISTRY

The life that the Lord Jesus lived on earth was not only sinless. It was perfect. His words were perfect. His thoughts were perfect and His actions were perfect. Everything that He did was not only in the perfect will of God, it was the perfect will of God. There was no way in which God could improve upon the life that Jesus lived on earth. This life was not lived in that way because He was the Son of God. In fact, He did not use His divinity to live His life on earth. When He left heaven to come on earth, He put aside all His rights and privileges as God. All the power that was manifested on earth, was power that He received from God in His condition as man. The Bible says, "*Although he was a Son, he learned obedience through what he suffered; and being made perfect he became the source of eternal salvation to all who obey him*" *(Hebrews 5:8-9). Again the Word says, "For it was fitting that he, for whom and by whom all things exist, in bringing many sons to glory, should make the pioneer of their salvation perfect through suffering*" (Hebrews 2:10). The Lord Jesus was thus perfected through suffering. The cries, the loud cries and the tears, which were an integral part of His daily dynamic encounters with God, were part of the painful but necessary process of His perfection. He learnt to know God's will each morning and He submitted to God's will each morning. When He said in Gethsemane, "*Yet not what I will but what thou wilt*" (Mark 14:36), He was saying something that He had said many times before, and perhaps every morning, as He sought and received God's will for each situation of the day before Him.

So each morning He presented His will to the Father. (As a man, Jesus had His own will). The Father showed Him His (the Father's) will and He put His aside and took the Father's will. He then went into the day with only the Father's will on His heart. The conflicts of wills were settled during the morning intercourse, and throughout the day there was perfect harmony, since there was only one will to do.

Because of this impact of His encounter with God on His will, all that flowed from Him was perfect. All that flowed from Him was as God wanted it to be. He could be loving to a sinner and He could be stern to a hypocrite. He was fearless. He was doing the Father's will and had nothing of His own to lose. What reason had He to be afraid of anyone? The Father was backing Him 100%, could anyone do to Him what was not permitted by His Father? So His character was perfect.

What about His ministry? It, too, was deeply affected by the morning encounters with God. I can imagine that the Father showed Him all that He was going to face in the day and gave Him clear instructions on what He was to do in each case. The Father would tell Him, "You will be asked this question by so, so, and so. This is the answer You shall give. A blind man will come to You today seeking healing. This is what You shall do to heal him. A cripple will come to You. You will heal him by saying the following words ...... A demon possessed man will be brought to You. You will deliver him by saying ....... There will be thousands of people needing to be fed. You will reach out to them by doing the following ....... So the Father showed Him all that was to happen in the day. He also showed Him what He was to do and He gave Him all the authority that would be needed to ensure that every proclamation of Jesus' came to pass.

So the Lord Jesus could honestly say, "*My food is to do the will of him who sent me, and to accomplish his work*" (John 4:34).


"*I can do nothing on my own authority; as I hear, I judge; and my judgment is just, because I seek not my own will but the will of him who sent me*" (John 5:30).

"*For I have come down from heaven, not to do my will but the will of him who sent me*" (John 6:38).

"*I glorified thee on earth, having accomplished the work which thou gavest me to do*" (John 17:4).

Having everything from the Father every morning, is there any wonder that He was a total success? Is there any wonder that He was tempted in every way but He did not sin? Is it surprising that He could ask, "Which one of you accuses me of sin?" and not one of His enemies raised his hand against Him? Is there any surprise at the fact that He healed all the sick who were brought to Him on all occasions? Do we wonder at the fact that He cast out all the demons that came His way? Is it not understandable that the dead came back to life as He bid them do; that trees "died" at His word; that water turned into wine at His word; that bread was multiplied at His command; that weaklings like Peter became bold and powerful ministers of the New Covenant, that a wretch like me was saved, nearly two thousand years after His last morning meditation on earth, because of the power and victory of His death and resurrection?

It all fits in. It all makes sense. He received authority from the Father in heaven. He renewed it every day in the morning. He received the master-plan of His ministry in heaven. He reviewed it each morning with His Father. And so all was a success.

The morning encounter between the Lord Jesus and the Lord of all glory was an absolute must for His life and His ministry. It is an absolute must for the life and ministry of all who will be like Him in character and service. It is optional for all who have chosen to fail.


Follow His example.

Make it a must for your own life and ministry. Amen.

# CHAPTER 2

# THE BIBLE AND DAILY DYNAMIC ENCOUNTERS WITH GOD - 1

"*The law of the Lord is perfect, reviving the soul;*
*the testimony of the Lord is sure, making wise the simple;*
*the precepts of the Lord are right, rejoicing the heart;*
*the commandment of the Lord is pure,*
*enlightening the eyes;*
*the fear of the Lord is clean, enduring for ever;*
*the ordinances of the Lord are true,*
*and righteous altogether.*
*More to be desired are they than gold,*
*even much fine gold, sweeter also than honey*
*and drippings of the honeycomb.*
*Moreover by them is thy servant warned;*
*in keeping them there is great reward.*
*But who can discern his errors?*
*Clear thou me from hidden faults.*
*Keep back thy servant also from presumptuous sins,*
*let them not have dominion over me!*
*Then I shall be blameless and innocent of great transgression.*
*Let the words of my mouth and the meditation of my heart*
*be acceptable in thy sight,*
*O Lord, my rock and my redeemer*" (Psalm 19:7-14).

We can say that the main method by which God speaks to man is through His Word - the Bible, and the main way through which man speaks to God is through prayer. When a man reads God's Word and hears God speaking to Him through it and he responds to what he has heard through prayer and obedience, fellowship with God is established. Once established, fellowship is maintained by the same method by which it was initially established, that is, by God speaking to man through His Word and man responding through prayer and obedience.

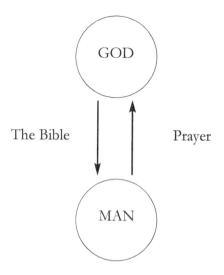

*The place of the Bible in daily dynamic encounters with God*

The Word of God is all important.

We shall look at this very briefly.

## GOD'S ESTIMATION OF HIS WORD

The Bible is as great and as important as God esteems it. What is God's estimation of His Word?

God has raised His Word to such a position of supreme authority that He "submits" absolutely to it. He obeys everything written in His Word. He said in His Word that He would smite the shepherd and the sheep would scatter. That shepherd happened to be His only begotten Son, and He refused to spare Him. He submitted to, "It is written." God cannot disobey His Word. It is one of the very few things that will endure for ever - that cannot be altered. The Lord said, "*Heaven and earth will pass away, but my word will not pass away*" (Matthew 24:35).

## THE PSALMIST'S ESTIMATION OF GOD'S WORD

God's Word was everything to the Psalmist. A few psalms will show this fact very clearly. He wrote: "*Blessed are those whose walk is blameless, who walk in the law of the Lord. Blessed are those who keep his testimonies, who seek him with their whole heart, who also do no wrong, but walk in his way! Thou hast commanded thy precepts, to be kept diligently. O that my ways may be steadfast in keeping thy statutes! Then I shall not be put to shame, having my eyes fixed on all thy commandments. I will praise thee with an upright heart, when I learn thy righteous ordinances. I will observe thy statutes, O forsake me not utterly*" (Psalm 119:1-8).

He continued to write, "*Thy testimonies are my delight, they are my counsellors. My soul cleaves to the dust; revive me according to thy word! When I told of my ways thou didst answer me; teach me thy statutes! Make me understand the way of thy precepts, and I will meditate on thy wondrous works. My soul melts away for sorrow; strengthen me according to thy word! Put false ways far from me; and graciously teach me thy law*" (Psalm 119:24-29).

So the Psalmist talks of God's Word as His law, commandments, statutes, ordinances and Word. He valued the Word of the Lord. He sought it and he kept it.

## THE IMPORTANCE OF GOD'S WORD
## TO THE BELIEVER

The Psalmist said, "*Thy word is a lamp to my feet and a light to my path*" (Psalm 119:105). This means that the believer needs the Word both to see his way and his direction. He also needs the Word to be rightly related to other believers and other people.

The Word is like God's road map to heaven. Without it, going astray is obvious.

The Word is important in sanctification. The Bible says, "*How can a young man keep his way pure? By guarding it according to thy Word*"

*(Psalm 119:9). It again says, "I have laid up thy word in my heart, that I might not sin against thee"* (Psalm 119:11). The Lord of glory prayed, *"Sanctify them in the truth; thy word is truth"* (John 17:17).

The Word is indispensable for a knowledge of God - His being, His thoughts, His ways, and so on. A believer needs the Word of God for his spiritual maintenance, just as he needs food for his physical upkeep.

Those who know the Word make spiritual progress.

## LOVING GOD AND LOVING GOD'S WORD

The Bible is a love letter written by the Lord to His beloved. Those who love Him love His Word. Those who do not love Him do not love His Word. In fact, one way of knowing who the lovers of God are, is to find out who love His Word. Those who love His Word read it and re-read it. They memorise parts of it and find their greatest pleasure in meditating upon it. The Psalmist was a great lover of God. His love for God is manifested by his love for His Word. He said,

- *"In the way of thy testimonies I delight as much as in riches"* (Psalm 119:14).

- *"I will delight in thy statutes, I will not forget thy word"* (Psalm 119:16).

- *"Open my eyes, that I may behold wondrous things out of thy law"* (Psalm 119:18).

- *"My soul is consumed with longing for thy ordinances all the time"* (Psalm 119:20).

- *"Thy testimonies are my delight; they are my counsellors"* (Psalm 119:24).

- *"I cleave to thy testimonies; O Lord, let me not be put to shame"* (Psalm 119:31).

- *"Oh, how I love thy law! It is my meditation all the day"* (Psalm 119:97).
- *"I find my delight in thy commandments which I love"* (Psalm 119:47).
- *"I revere thy commandments, which I love, and I will meditate on thy statutes"* (Psalm 119:48).
- *"The law of thy mouth is better to me than thousands of gold and silver pieces"* (Psalm 119:72).
- *"How sweet are thy words to my taste, sweeter than honey to my mouth"* (Psalm 119: 103).
- *"Thy testimonies are my heritage for ever; yea, they are the joy of my heart"* ( Psalm 119:111).
- *"Therefore I love thy commandments above gold, fine gold"* (Psalm 119:127).
- *"With open mouth I pant, because I long for thy commandments"* (Psalm 119:131).
- *"Consider how I love thy precepts"* (Psalm 119:159).
- *"My soul keeps thy testimonies, I love them exceedingly"* (Psalm 119:167).

Do you see his attitude towards the Word of the Lord? He delighted in it as in riches in the beginning of his walk with God. Later on, as his love for the Lord grew, he found the law of the Lord better to him than thousands of gold and silver pieces, and after yet more progress, he found that he loved God's commandments above gold, fine gold. He was indeed a lover of God's Word. He delighted in it. His soul was consumed with longing for God's Word. He cleaved to it. He revered it. It was sweeter than honey to his mouth. It was the joy of his heart. He panted for it, longed for it, and finally loved it exceedingly.

It is interesting to notice that the Psalmist loved the Lord in the same way that he loved His Word. He said of the Lord, *"One thing have I asked of the Lord, that I will seek after; that I may dwell in the house of the Lord all the days of my life, to behold the beauty of the Lord, and to inquire in his temple"* (Psalm 27:4).

*"As a hart longs for flowing streams, so longs my soul for thee, O God. My soul thirsts for God, for the living God. When shall I come and behold the face of God?"* (Psalm 42:1-2).

*"O God, thou art my God, I seek thee, my soul thirsts for thee; my flesh faints for thee, as in a dry and weary land where no water is"* (Psalm 63:1).

*"How lovely is thy dwelling place, O Lord of hosts! My soul longs, yea, faints for the courts of the Lord; my heart and flesh sing for joy to the living God"* (Psalm 84:1-2).

*"I stretch out my hands to thee, my soul thirsts for thee, like a parched land"* (Psalm 143:6).

## WHY IS THERE SUCH A SHORTAGE OF LOVERS OF GOD'S WORD TODAY?

We must admit in all honesty that there are very few believers in the church in our day who know anything near what the Psalmist experienced with regards to God's Word. For many believers, the Word of God is something boring. It is something that they do not spontaneously flow to. They do not desire it always. It is not sweet to them. It is not their joy. It is not more precious to them than honey. It is not more meaningful to them than money. They can neglect it for days, whereas they could not neglect other things that mean more to them. What is the reason for this abnormality? I think there are a number of reasons for it.

The first reason I can think of is that they do not love the Lord. The lack of love for His Word is a manifestation of the fact that they do not love Him. The Psalmist burned after the Lord. He also burned after His Word. He said, *"With open mouth I pant, because I long for thy commandments*" (Psalm 119:131). He also said, "*I stretch out my hands to thee; my soul thirsts for thee like a parched land*" (Psalm 143:6).

We ask, "Why is there no love for God in the hearts of God's children? Have they never loved Him? Has their love grown cold?" I think that there are some who are His who have never really loved Him in any deep way. Their commitment to Him has been legal and logical, but they have never been swept off their feet in a total love affair with Him that involved their spirits, souls and bodies. They also love the Word intellectually. However, there are others who once loved the Lord very deeply and very totally at the beginning of their relationship with Him. He was everything to them. They gave Him their all without reservation and they obeyed Him in everything. They were content, fully satisfied in Him. Everyone else and everything else was secondary. His commands were gladly obeyed. His Word was their delight. They read it and reread it and enjoyed it. I remember a few years ago, when a young disciplined man found the Lord. He locked himself up and in three days, he had finished reading the entire New Testament. He loved the Lord and told everyone about Him. His love for the Lord was manifested in His love for God's Word. We thank the Lord for people like that. The only problem is that many who started with the same kind of love for the Lord and His Word have not continued. I think the problem is that when they found the Lord, they gave Him all their hearts. They could have said with the Psalmist that there was no one else and nothing else that they desired on earth besides the Lord or in addition to Him. The Lord was enough for them. He was all they needed. He possessed them and He was their joy and He spoke to them through His Word. The Bible was like a love letter written personally to them by the Lord, and they just loved it.

However, they soon began to be pre-occupied with the cares of the world. I am not saying that they fell into any terrible sin. They began to desire the things of the world slowly and one after another. Their hearts were taken away by the cares of the world, the desires for riches, the desires for the pleasures of life; the desires for other things came in and choked the heart and ruined the love of the Lord and His Word. The things that convert a lover of the Lord and His Word into an insipid believer may be legitimate. It may be the desire for marriage, children, education, property and so on. However, each of these things comes with its own problems. A car brings with it additional fears. It may be worry as to where to park it so that it is safe from thieves; what will happen with the insurance if funds are low; what will happen if there is an accident. Yes, a car may be permissible, but the problems that it brings occupy a person so that his heart is no longer as available to God and His Word as before! Think about the legitimate issue of marriage. The Bible says, "*Yet those who marry will have worldly troubles*" (1 Corinthians 7:28). Think of a young man who is unmarried. His cry is, "I wish I had a wife." Then he has a wife. Then another cry is: "Will the marriage work? Shall I satisfy my wife? Will she satisfy me?" That problem may be partly solved. Then a third problem may come up. It is the question of children. "Shall we be able to have children?" If children come, then there is the problem of what sexes they are. Some are worried because they have only boys and others are worried because they have only girls. Others are dissatisfied because the first child was not of the sex that they desired. Then the problem may be that they do not know how to prevent too many children from being born. They may worry about the child's performance in primary school or worry as to whether the child will pass the entrance examination for entry into secondary school. They may worry as to whether the child will pass in the right list. Then they will later be worried as to whether their child will pass the "Ordinary" Level examination. Then they may worry as to whether the child will be of the science or arts discipline. Then they will worry as to whether the child will pass the "Advanced" Level Examination and where he will enrol for university education, then worry about the matter of his having a job upon graduation, whether he will find the right partner, and so on and so forth. There is no end to possible areas of worrying, and each worry interferes with the heart's love for God. Is that what has happened to your heart?

Or is your problem a matter of sin? Sin will keep a person away from the Bible, just as the Bible will keep a person from sin. We know that the person who continues to do the things that God forbids will sooner or later find that his love for the Lord and His Word has grown cold. A Hymn writer wrote that by many deeds of shame we learn that love grows cold. The devil is not anxious to get believers to steal, to commit adultery or fornication in action. He just specialises in getting them to commit adultery in their hearts, gossip, lie in small ways, complain, and so on; and each of these is enough to block the heart from loving the Lord and loving His Word. He knows that the grosser sins are not likely to work; for even if a believer were to be mad enough to commit adultery in action, he would soon repent with dust and ashes and be restored to vital fellowship with the Lord and His Word, whereas few ever consider an adulterous thought as causing equal ruin, and, consequently, few ever really repent deeply and seek restoration to the Lord. So he (Satan) accomplishes his purpose through those sins which, although equally dangerous, are taken lightly by many believers.

There is another reason why believers do not maintain their first love for the Lord and His Word. The Lord will only continue to talk through His Word to those who obey Him. Many believers read the Word of the Lord but they are not pre-occupied with obeying it. After repeated acts of disobedience they find that the Lord no longer speaks to them when they approach His Word, and, as the Lord ceases to speak, the Bible becomes a dead and, finally, a closed book.

The Psalmist knew that he could not trust his heart on its own to obey the Word of the Lord. He needed to discipline it, and confessed:

1.    "*I incline my heart to perform thy statutes forever, to the end*" (Psalm 119:112).

2.    "*Therefore I direct my steps by all thy precepts; I hate every false way*" (Psalm 119:128).

He did not only find discipline necessary.

He found obedience necessary. He said,

1.    "*Thy testimonies are wonderful, therefore my soul keeps them*" (Psalm 119:129).

2.    "*Redeem me from man's oppression that I may keep thy precepts*" (Psalm 119:134).

3.    "*Many are my persecutors and my adversaries, but I do not swerve from thy testimonies*" (Psalm 119:157).

4.    "*I hope in thy salvation, O Lord, and I do thy commandments*" (Psalm 119:166).

5.    "*My soul keeps thy testimonies, I love them exceedingly*" (Psalm 119:167).

6.    "*I keep thy precepts and testimonies, for all my ways are before thee*" (Psalm 119:168).

As he obeyed the Word, his love for the Lord and His Word grew. All who have lost their first love for the Lord must go to the Lord as a matter of urgency and say to Him, "Lord, I have lost my first love for You and for Your Word." Or they may pray, saying, "Lord, I have never loved You and Your Word. Lord, where did I go wrong? Was it some sin? What was the matter, Lord?" They must seek the Lord until He talks to them, shows them what is wrong, helps them to correct it, and then be restored to loving Him and loving His Word. They must, however, seek Him with their whole heart. If not, they will not find Him. The Psalmist said, "*Blessed are those who keep his testimonies, who seek him with their whole heart*"

(Psalm 119:2). and "*With my whole heart I cry; answer me, O Lord! I will keep thy statutes*" (Psalm 119:145). The Lord said, "*I love those who love me, and those who seek me diligently find me*" (Proverbs 8:17).

One last thing that we want to mention about the matter of not loving God's Word is this: There are many who do not love His Word because they do not understand it. They love Him, but because they do not understand His Word, they find themselves increasingly separated from it. The Psalmist knew about this possibility and so he prayed asking that the Lord should teach him and cause him to understand the Word. He said to the Lord:

1.  "*Open my eyes, that I may behold wondrous things out of thy law*" (Psalm 119:18).

2.  "*I am a sojourner on earth, hide not thy commandments from me*" (Psalm 119:19).

3.  "*When I told of my ways, thou didst answer me; teach me thy statutes*" (Psalm 119:26).

4.  "*Make me understand the way of thy precepts, and I will meditate on thy wondrous works*" (Psalm 119:27).

5.  "*Put false ways far from me, and graciously teach me thy law*" (Psalm 119:29).

6.  "*I will run in the way of thy commandments when thou enlargest my understanding*" (Psalm 119:32).

7.  "*Teach me, O Lord, the way of thy statutes; I will keep it to the end. Give me understanding, that I may keep thy law and observe it with my whole heart*" (Psalm 119:34).

8.  "*Incline my heart to thy testimonies, and not to gain*" (Psalm 119:36).

9.  "*Accept my offering of praise, O Lord, and teach me thy ordinances*" (Psalm 119:108).

10. "*I am thy servant; give me understanding, that I may know thy testimonies*" (Psalm 119:125).

11.  *"Thy testimonies are righteous for ever; give me understanding that I may live"* (Psalm 119:144).

12.  *"Let my cry come before thee, O Lord; give me understanding according to thy Word"* (Psalm 119:169).


Knowing, therefore, the need for divine enabling in order that the Word may be understood and obeyed, the Psalmist turned desperately to God. He leaned on Him and trusted in Him. He asked. He supplicated. He cried, and the Lord heard him. He was given a living understanding of God's Word and also enabled to obey. In this way, his love for the Word of the Lord abided.

The same pathway is open to all who want to maintain their love for God's Word. They, too, should confess their ignorance to Him. They should cry to Him. They should insist that He hear them and that He answer them. They should continue to insist and they should refuse to take any delay or a "No" for an answer. If they insist and put their heart right with Him as they continue to insist, He will hear from heaven, come to their aid and they shall be blessed indeed.

Be one such! Start today.


Amen.

# CHAPTER 3

# THE BIBLE AND DAILY DYNAMIC ENCOUNTERS WITH GOD - 2

1.  Master, speak! Thy servant heareth,
    Waiting for Thy gracious Word;
    Longing for Thy voice that cheereth,
    Master, let it now be heard.
    I am list'ning, Lord, for Thee:
    What hast Thou to say to me?

2.  Speak to me by name, O Master,
    Let me know it is to me;
    Speak, that I may follow faster,
    With a step more firm and free,
    Where the Shepherd leads the flock,
    In the shadow of the Rock.

3.  Master, speak! Tho' least and lowest
    Let me not unheard depart;
    Master, speak! for Oh, Thou knowest
    All the yearning of my heart.
    Knowest all its truest need;
    Speak! and make me blest indeed.

4.  Master, speak! and make me ready,
    When Thy voice is truly heard,
    With obedience glad and steady,
    Still to follow ev'ry word.
    I am list'ning, Lord, for Thee;
    Master, speak, Oh, speak to me!
    (Redemption Songs No. 835)

## DIFFERENT APPROACHES TO BIBLE MEDITATION

In Bible meditation the following possibilities are opened to the believer:

a. Long passages,

b. Short passages,

c. A verse,

d. Part of a verse,

e. A word,

f. A theme,

g. A character.

A person may find that he needs to read a long passage before he finds what will meet his spiritual need for that day. He should go ahead that way. Later on, he will find that a short passage has enough food to meet his need. Then he may find one verse so pregnant with food and application for his life that he needs many days to get to the root of things. Let us take one such verse an for example, or a group of such verses together. "*Now the works of the flesh are plain: fornication, impurity, licentiousness, idolatry, sorcery, enmity, strife, anger, selfishness, dissension, party spirit, envy, drunkenness, carousing, and the like. I warn you as I warned you before, that those who do such things shall not inherit the kingdom of God*" (Galatians 5:19-21). A person can meditate on these verses for many days. He will take each thing that is mentioned in turn and ask God to show him if it is found in his life. The Bible says that the works are plain, but what is plain to most people may not be plain to others. The wise person will not jump over the issues and say that they are not for him. After all, they are from a letter that was written to believers. It is only reality to think that some believers do such things or that there are people who think that they are believers and do such things, whereas they are not. Since the Bible says that those who do such things will not enter the kingdom of God, should everyone not look at the list carefully? Take the matter of adultery. The one who is looking at the list will possibly ask, "Did I commit adultery before I came to the Lord?" If the answer is, "yes," he will ask himself, *"With whom did I commit it?"* He will further ask *"Did I clearly repent to the Lord? Did I truly repent to the person? Did I forsake the sin? Did I carry out restitution?" He will examine each question carefully and ask God to show him things as they are. He will not want to deceive himself. After he has settled all that took place before he believed, he will ask, "Have I committed adultery since I believed?" As he asks himself the question, he will remember two passages of the Bible which say, "But I say to you that every one who looks at a woman lustfully has already committed adultery with her in his heart"* (Matthew 5:28). *"Do not desire her beauty in your heart, and do not let her capture you with her eye lashes"* (Proverbs 6:25). So if you have once committed adultery with any woman in your heart, if you have once desired her beauty in your heart, then you are in trouble. You are among those who have been warned that they will not see the kingdom of God. You will see immediately that since God looks at the heart, adultery in the heart is adultery before God, and it is as disastrous as adultery in action. You will then make a list of the people with whom you have ever committed adultery in your heart and repent to the Lord, confess your sin and seek permanent deliverance. You can see then that one word, "adultery" may be the subject of many meditations. It can also be seen that for the person who wants to examine things deeply before God and let the Spirit of God show him the true condition of his heart, the three verses of Galatians chapter 5:19-21 may be the subject of searching and enriching meditations for many days and perhaps weeks.

A person may also decide to meditate on the conflict between Israel and the Philistines that is recorded in 1 Samuel chapter 17. It is quite obvious that this will take many mornings of real meditation to exhaust. He may want to hold the passage together; yet he will want to take it portion by portion for meditation. For example, he may want to meditate on the first twelve verses and see the nature of Goliath's size, armour, challenge, provocation, and the impact that it had on the children of Israel. He will then work out how this affects him. He will see if there are some Goliaths in his life or ministry and see how he is reacting to them. He may then next meditate on the person of David and his appearance on the battle field. He may then look at David's introduction to Goliath and his attitude to him, work out the application of faith in spiritual warfare, and see what areas in his life need to come under a walk of faith. He may then meditate on David's offer to face the Philistines, and study David's credentials for the task. Such meditation may lead him to examine his own daily faithfulness before God, and see what type of credentials he has gathered for himself. He may then want to study Saul's armour and David's rejection of it in order to see the need not to depend on the arm of flesh. He will surely let the Lord show him in what areas of his life he is depending on the arm of flesh and, if he is sensitive, he will do what David did with the armour of Saul - put it aside. He may next meditate on the weapons that David chose for the battle and see the availability of such weapons for his own conflict with the enemy. He may then finally meditate on the conflict, defeat, death of Goliath, overthrow of the Philistines and the final triumph of David and Israel, drawing lessons on God's provision for warfare for him, faith in warfare, the overthrow of enemies and the matter of winning battles for the household of God.

How long he will take will depend on the depth of his fellowship with God, his capacity to receive from the Lord, his ability to apply the Word to his own life, his spiritual experience and the amount of time that is available for each meditation.

Even in the life of one believer in the same period of time, there will be variations in his approach to different meditations, depending on what the Lord wants to talk to him about and his willingness to face the light of God.

Spiritual babes will approach a passage differently from spiritual adults. The lovers of the Lord will approach a passage differently from those who do not love Him.  Those who have two to three hours for their meditation will approach a passage differently from those who have only thirty minutes to spare.

Those who must meet God will approach a passage differently from those who just want to carry out the formality of having meditated, possibly for the whole purpose of pleasing some human being.

You will find that things change as you make spiritual progress. You should be forward looking in your approach to meditation. You should be open to the Lord to lead you. You should ask Him to lead you. You should learn from others, but you should wait on the Lord and He will lead you and guide you. He is willing. He is able. He is the One you want to know. He is the One you want to encounter. Let Him lead and  you shall be blessed.

## HOW TO BEGIN PERSONAL MEDITATION: PRACTICAL CONSIDERATIONS

### a) A covenant with God.

Each believer should enter into a covenant with God as to when he will meet God every morning. The time of that meeting should be prayerfully thought out and prayed about. When it is settled, it should be adhered to come rain, or shine. The believer should then tell the Lord the time when they will meet each morning. From that time on, the believer must make sure that he is at his appointment with God.

If a believer settles it with God that they will meet each other at 4.00 am, it means that even if because of some unforeseen events the believer could only go to bed at 1.00 am, he would still be up for his appointment with God. If he goes to bed at 2.00 am, he will rise up for the appointment at 4.00 am. If he finds that he has not yet slept by 4.00, he will not go to bed. It is his appointment time. He must meet his God. Sleep must wait. God cannot wait. The fact that many believers make appointments with God and do not keep them is most worrying. It should not be so. Can you imagine that our Head of State makes an appointment with any of his subjects at, say, 2.00 am and that one will not be there? I am very sure that the one who is invited would consider it a great privilege. He would not bother about the time. He would be full of joy that the Head of State has offered to see him. He would consider it a great honour and would prepare for it long before the time. He would go to the Presidency well ahead of time. He would say, "I must go long before the time, so that if some unexpected event, like having a flat tyre, should occur on my way there, I should still be in time; for I cannot afford to keep the Head of State waiting." The joy of meeting the Head of State would cause sleep to forsake him or he would make sure that he sleeps long before the appointment time. During morning meditation the believer is meeting not just an earthly Head of State. He is meeting the King of all the universe. The Head of State of all heads of states is the one who will be in audience. How can anyone keep Him waiting? How can anyone even sleep when he has such an appointment? Should the very thought of it not fill the believer with ecstasy? Should this not be the one event of the believer's day? Should he not look forward to it more than a bride looks forward to her wedding day?

It is painful to know that believers wake up, do not meet God, eat their morning meals and run to their various occupations. God can be left aside, but not breakfast! Their appointments with their jobs are more compelling and more indispensable than their appointments with the King of kings. I do not know any nation on earth that treats its ruler with the same degree of contempt that the citizens of heaven treat their God. It is most sad. I do not know any earthly ruler who has opted to make himself available to any one of his subjects at anytime that the subject wants. The King of heaven and earth has done that but Oh, how lightly we take Him!

We need sanity to return to the church of the First Born. We need a new breed of believers who have even the slightest respect for God in their hearts. Such will say to themselves, "No meeting with God, no meeting with man. No meeting with God, no meeting with food. No meeting with God, no going to work, and so on." Then they will ensure that they meet God first, transact the most important business on earth and come out in the strength of that transaction to carry out all the other businesses. They will do it out of love and loyalty to the Lord. They will do it also out of sheer necessity, for they know that the days in which God is given the first place in the morning, are also the best for all other relationships and all other businesses. Martin Luther said, "I have so much work to do today that I must spend the first three hours in prayer." May we all follow his example and put God first!

### b) **Being awake**

Some believers are completely awake immediately they come out of bed. Others are not so completely awake. In order to meditate properly, you need to be fully awake. I make the following suggestions. When you wake up, do the following:

1.   Shout,"Praise the Lord, praise the Lord!"

2.   Say aloud, "Good morning, my blessed Lord and Saviour."

3.   Say aloud, "This is the day that You have made. I will rejoice and be glad in it."

4.   Wash your face if you need to.

5.   Drink a cup of tea if you really need it for really becoming awake.

6.   Jump up several times, praising the Lord with each jump.

You should be fully awake after some or all of these activities. You are now ready to move to the place where you will meet your God and His Word.

### c) **Recording material.**

You are coming to meet God. He is going to speak to you. If He means much to you, you will want to keep a record of everything He says to you. You will, therefore, ensure that you come to your meeting with Him with a good note-book and a pen, and, of course, your Bible. The type of note-book that you will bring along will reflect something of how seriously you take the One you are going to encounter, and how seriously you plan to take what He will say to you. If you do not take Him seriously, you can bring rough sheets or some twenty-page note-book which you will discard with ease. If you consider that He will say things to you that are of eternal consequence and that you may need to refer to in the future, then you should take the type of note-book with you, to your appointment with Him, that you will be able to keep for many years to come. You should also ensure that you have a good pen.

The pen, Bible, and note-book should be put together the day before; so that when it is time for them to be used, they are available. It can be very disturbing to want to write and then find out that there is no pen around.

### d) **A place for meeting God.**

The Lord Jesus sought a quiet place and withdrew there to meet His God. You, too, should find a quiet place. If there is a quiet room in the house to which you can withdraw, you should do so. If there is no place that is specially quiet, you should ask the Lord to shut out the noise so that you will have quiet.

## e)Time for meeting God.

If the Head of State invites you for a discussion, he will normally be the one who will determine how long the discussion will be. The King of heaven is different. He is prepared to give us all the time that we need. The question is, "How much time do we need?" The amount of time that we need depends on the relationship that already exists between us and Him. When two strangers meet, ten minutes spent together may seem like an eternity. However, when lovers meet, many hours roll away so quickly before they realise it. When I first gave my life to the Lord Jesus twenty years ago, I found that thirty minutes were enough for my daily encounters with Him. At the moment, after two hours, I find that I am just finishing my meditation and need another hour to pray through the things raised. If it were possible to have four hours for my daily dynamic encounters with God, I would find my need well supplied. Unfortunately, at the moment, I am only able to afford two or three hours daily. My counsel to you is that if fifteen minutes are enough for you, do not imitate someone and spend two hours before your Bible yawning and feeling miserable. Thank God that your needs are met in fifteen minutes. As you go on in your walk with Him, the quality of the intimacy will make the need for more time necessary, and you will yourself gladly increase the time that you are spending before Him each morning.

Do not say that you do not have time. You have all the time that you want to pay the price for. If you want three hours, wake up at 3.00 am and you will have the time from 3.00 to 6.00 am to meet Him, and then you will have enough time for family worship before you prepare and go to work. If you need two hours, you will wake up at 4.00, and if you need one hour, you will plan to wake up at 5.00 am. Your hunger for God will determine the time you wake up and the time that you spend with Him each day. The time that you spend with Him each day will in the long run affect:

your character,

your ministry, and

your rank in heaven.

Be wise to decide carefully.

## HOW TO BEGIN PERSONAL MEDITATION: SPIRITUAL CONSIDERATIONS

### a) **Empty Yourself.**

It is possible to come for the time of meeting God in the morning and be unprepared to meet Him because of too many things that are filling your head and perhaps your heart. You should lay aside all such things and come to the Lord with a heart and a head that are able to receive what He will say to you. If you find difficulties in doing it, ask the Lord to help you. If a particular thing continues to hover in your mind, pray specifically about it, asking the Lord to take it away. If it still remains, it may be something from the enemy and you should take authority over it in the name of the Lord Jesus and ask it to depart forthwith. It will depart and your mind will be clear and settled to begin your meditation.

You also need to empty yourself of your pre-occupations, be they spiritual or material. You should ask the Lord to help you to forget the success of the day before and any mighty way in which God might have used you. You will realise that if you had a good meal the day before and the plates were not washed, they will not be good enough for the next meal to be served in. They are remains of what was good for the time past, but they are not good for now. The plates must be washed so that the fresh food can be served in them. You should also ask the Lord to empty your mind of your former understanding of the passage which you will be meditating upon. Without that emptying, it may be difficult for the Lord to give you something new from that passage, because your mind is bound to your previous opinion about the message it contains. You should ask the Lord to deliver you from all the prejudices of the past; so that you can hear His voice afresh. Do not force your problem on the passage. God has a message for you. He knows what you need. Be ready for it. Do not make the passage say what you want to hear.

## b) **Repentance.**

Sin will block God from speaking to you. It will block God from hearing you. The Psalmist said, "If I had cherished iniquity in my heart, the Lord would not have listened" (Psalm 66:18). The prophet said, "*Behold, the Lord's hand is not shortened, that it cannot save, or his ear dull, that it cannot hear; but your iniquities have made a separation between you and your God, and your sins have hid his face from you so that he does not hear. For your hands are defiled with blood and your fingers with iniquity; your lips have spoken lies, your tongue mutters wickedness*" (Isaiah 59:1-3).

The best thing is to spread your life before the Lord. If there is a sin that you have committed and you know it clearly, then you should repent, confess it to the Lord and forsake it permanently. If you do not know any sin in your life, it is best to ask the Lord to search your heart and show you sin that may be present in your life, but is not obvious to you. If there is sin in your life which you do not know about, your communion with God will be reduced, but it will not be hindered as when the sin is known but not confessed and forsaken.

You must be honest with God. If there is a sin in your life that you know about but you do not want to forsake and abandon, you should not bother to meditate. God will not talk to you. You may analyze His Word with your mind and deceive yourself, but God will not commune with someone who does not want to forsake the obvious sin in his life. Are you deceived into thinking that God will close His eyes to your sin and talk to you? You are only deceiving yourself.

It may be that your sin is that of lying or falsehood. Do not ignore it. It is big enough to take people to the lake of fire. The Bible says, "...and all liars, their lot shall be in the lake that burns with fire and sulphur, which is the second death" (Revelation 21:8). "*But nothing unclean shall enter it, nor anyone who practices abomination or falsehood, but only those whose names are written in the Lamb's book of life*" (Revelation 21:27). If you have told a lie, exaggerated a story, given a false impression or any other sin, you should repent and forsake the sin.

When you have repented of your sin, confessed and forsaken it, you should ask the Lord to forgive you and cleanse you. The Bible says, "*If we say we have no sin, we deceive ourselves, and the truth is not in us. If we confess our sins, he is faithful and just, and will forgive our sins and cleanse us from all unrighteousness. If we say that we have not sinned, we make him a liar, and his word is not in us*" (1 John 1:8-10).

You should accept God's forgiveness which He offers to you upon confession of your sin. To ask for forgiveness and yet to go about feeling sorry for yourself does not deepen your repentance. It deepens your self-love. God is not moved by self-love. He is not glorified by the remorse of those who continue to "feel broken" after He has forgiven and cleansed them.

### c) **Restitution.**

If the Holy Spirit leads you to carry out restitution about any sin which you committed and have repented of and forsaken, then you must obey Him. He may lead you to go and confess the lies that you told to those to whom you told them or to correct the false impression that you gave, by speaking the truth. Do not resist Him as He leads you in that direction. However, it must be Him leading you and not the legal code of someone else or some organisation. If He leads you to put something right with someone who is in the same house with you, wake the person up from sleep or go to him where he, too, is having his own encounter with God and put things right with him, and then come and continue your time with God. The Bible says, "*So if you are offering your gift at the altar, and there remember that your brother has something against you, leave your gift there before the altar and go; first be reconciled to your brother, and then come and offer your gift*" (Matthew 5:23-24). If the person to whom the restitution is to be made is not within reach, go on with your meditation, but labour to carry out restitution at the earliest opportunity. Remember that it is the Holy Spirit who is leading you to carry out the restitution. Do not resist Him. Do not try to deceive Him; for He cannot be deceived. You can only deceive yourself. Do not deceive yourself.

### d) **Being filled with the Holy Spirit.**

When you have settled the matter of sin in your life clearly with the Lord, or if the Lord shows you that there is no sin to bother about, you should move to the next step and be filled with the Holy Spirit. Only sin and unbelief can hinder the believer from being filled with the Holy Spirit. You have settled the matter of sin. You should believe the Lord to fill you with the Holy Spirit if you ask Him. The Bible says, "*If you then, who are evil know how to give good gifts to your children, how much more will the heavenly Father give the Holy Spirit to those who ask Him!*" (Luke 11:13). The Holy Spirit is received by faith upon asking at the beginning of the Spirit-filled life. He is received by faith upon asking on all subsequent occasions. If you ask believing, you should believe that you have been filled as you asked. Do not wait for any further manifestation before you believe. He may fill you and there will be manifestations that are noticeable by you, or He may fill you and there will be manifestations that are not. Believe that God has honoured His Word and your request and filled you as you asked. The Bible says, "*Therefore I tell you, whatsoever you ask in prayer, believe that you have received it, and it will be yours*" (Mark 11:24). You asked the Lord to fill you with the Holy Spirit. Believe that you have been filled and you will be filled.

You may ask why it is important that you be filled with the Holy Spirit before you approach the Word of God. The reason is that He, the Holy Spirit, is the Author of the Bible. Men wrote as He moved them to write. He is also the Master Teacher. If you are filled with Him, He will lead you readily to understand what He wrote and teach you how to apply it to your life. He will also lead you into deeper union with the Lord Jesus whom you love. In fact, only people who are indwelt by the Holy Spirit can understand the Bible, and only people who are filled with Him can get the most out of it. Labour to be one of those who get the most out of it.

### e) Faith that God will speak to you.

You are coming to meet God through His Word and through prayer. Believe that He will be there and that He will speak to you. Why should He not speak to you? He is your Father. He delights to speak to you. You should believe that He will do so. Do not say to yourself, "God will not speak to me. I am too unworthy." That is a negative confession and it will not help you. By speaking that way, you are manifesting unbelief. Without faith, it is impossible to please God. You are coming to seek Him. Believe His Word that He rewards those who diligently seek Him. He will reward you in many ways. One of them is by speaking to you. You should believe that He will speak to you and you should confess it. Say aloud, "The Father loves me. He will speak to me today as I meditate upon His Word." So, come with a spirit of expectancy. Come determined to meet Him. Come with a settled attitude that unless He speaks to you, you will not go away from His presence. The Lord loves people who come with such pure and holy determination, and He does not allow them to depart unheard and unblessed.

### f) Commitment to obey

The Lord is going to speak to you. Commit yourself to obey before you enter into His presence. Tell Him, "Lord, speak to Your servant. He will obey You regardless of what that obedience will cost him." *With those words, you have vowed to obey the Lord. He will speak to you as someone who has committed himself to obey. Make sure that you keep your vow.* The Bible says, "When you vow a vow to God, do not delay paying it; for he has no pleasure in fools. Pay what you vow" (Ecclesiastes 5:4).

"*Praise is due to thee, O God, in Zion, and to thee shall vows be performed*" (Psalm 65:1).

"*Make your vows to the Lord your God, and perform them; let all around him bring gifts to him who is to be feared*" (Psalm 76:11).

"*Offer to God a sacrifice of thanksgiving, and pay your vows to the Most High*" (Psalm 50:14).

### g) **Choosing the passage from which to meditate**

We strongly recommend that you should take a book of the Bible and meditate upon it from the beginning to the end. Or you should choose a section of the Bible which has a special theme and meditate on it from start to finish. You could meditate on the book of Genesis. Stay on it until you have finished it. Or you could meditate on the Gospel according to the apostle Matthew. Again we recommend that you should stay on it until you have meditated on the whole book. Or you may meditate on the Sermon on the Mount (Matthew chapters 5-7) or on the Lord and His own in private (John 13-17) or you could meditate on an epistle like Romans or Philippians. You might also meditate on special chapters like Psalm 119 or 1 Corinthians 13. It is, of course, understood that some of these books or passages will take weeks and perhaps many months to finish. Go systematically from day to day. Do not choose your passages at random. Do not meditate on Monday on a verse in Genesis, on Tuesday, on a passage in Numbers and on Wednesday, on a passage in Revelation. God is not the Author of confusion. We insist that you should follow a book or a passage systematically. Unless you do so, you are likely to be confused. Do not bother if one book takes many months. Last year, I meditated on the epistle to the Philippians. I started meditating on the first verse of the book on 9th October and I finished meditating on the last verses (Philippians 4:19-23) on 31st December. You may not stay so long on one epistle, but please do stay until you have finished it. If you want to see what a man is like and you look at his head and then jump to his legs and then come back to his eyes and then jump to his fingers and then back to his nose, and so on, you will have a confused picture. Do not do that.

The story is told of someone who used to open his Bible at random, close his eyes and then place his finger on a verse and take that verse to be God's message for him for that day. One day, he placed his finger on the following verses one after another.

Matthew 27:5 "*And throwing down the pieces of silver in the temple, he departed, and he went and hanged himself.*"

Luke 10:37 "*....Go and do likewise.*"

John 13:27 "*....What you are going to do, do quickly.*"

If this man were to obey the "messages" that he had "received", he would have gone and hanged himself and he would have had to do it quickly!

My beloved brethren, follow the Bible systematically as you meditate upon it.

You may ask, "How am I to know where to start?" We suggest that you should ask the Holy Spirit to show you which book you should meditate on. He knows your needs in the days, weeks and months ahead. He also knows what He has in each book of the Bible. He will lead you to the book that will be best used to meet your needs. Personally, when I am half-way through a book, I begin to ask the Lord to guide me and show me which should be the second book on which I am to meditate. By the time I am through with the current book, He will have shown me what the next book should be. He will do the same for you.

There may be special times when the Lord will lead you to leave the book you are meditating on and go to another passage. If He leads you in that way, you should follow His leading. After you have received the special lesson that He sent you to that other passage for, you should come back and continue your systematic meditation on the book in which you were meditating before. However, before you move to another passage, make sure that you are being led by the Lord and not by your whims.

There will be times when, as you approach the Word, the Lord will talk to you directly on some serious matter. Be open to that, too, and do not resist His voice because of your systematic meditation. However, such occasions are the exception and not the rule. If they begin to be too frequent in such a way that you can no longer meditate on the Word, you are under demonic attack. You should seek ministry.

A sister once told me that the 'Lord' spoke to her every night for many hours. She said that she had written what He was telling her in many books until she was tired of writing, and that so much was the voice of 'God' talking to her that she could not sleep for days. It is immediately obvious that the one speaking to her was not the Lord. She needed ministry.

### h) **What of Bible Study aids?**

There are devotional aids like "My Utmost for His Highest," "Day by Day with Watchman Nee", and so on. We thank the Lord for such aids. However, they should not be used for morning meditation. You should come yourself to the Word and let God speak to you. He spoke to those who expressed what he said in those books. He wants to speak to you; so that you too can have your own "Day by Day with ... " You certainly want the original and not the copy. Go to God for something that is originally yours. In the last chapter, we shall make suggestions on how to use the meditations of others like the books we have mentioned above. They have their place. We, however, insist that in the morning, you should come yourself directly to the Bible and to the Lord. We say the same thing for commentaries, good as they may be. They are the comments of other people on the passage. Let God lead you to make your own commentary. It may not be as scholarly as theirs, but it will be original and it will be what the Lord is leading you directly into.

You may need a good dictionary to check up a word whose meaning you do not understand. Take a passage like Galatians 5:19-21. Some people may need a dictionary to find out the meaning of words like licentiousness, dissension, carousing... , before they can meditate properly on them. To refuse such help is folly.

### i) What version of the Bible should you use?

We recommend that you use the Bible that is written in the language that you understand the easiest. There is no need choosing a version that renders many things obscure to you. It may help to have two or three versions handy and read the passage from all of them. This may help you to grasp the message clearly. If you find that many versions confuse you, stick to one. Personally, I use just one version for my meditation in the morning, but I use many versions for Bible study.

### j) Is there any difference between Bible meditation and Bible study?

Yes, there is a difference. Bible study aims at Biblical knowledge. Bible meditation aims at spiritual knowledge. The first goal of Bible study is to understand the passage. You analyze it. You compare it with other passages, comparing Scripture with Scripture. You use all the commentaries possible and every other aid. You obtain something for your spirit as well, but that only comes out of the study.

In Bible meditation, you come to the Word of God as a child and ask God to give you something from it to nourish your spirit and direct your path. You read it and you wait on God and on God alone to speak to you out of the passage. You open up your whole life to the message in the passage, and God encourages, guides, directs or rebukes you as need may be. You leave morning meditation having met God and having heard from Him, and you go out into the day to obey and apply what He said to you. In Bible study, you deal with the Bible as the Logos of God. In morning meditation, you come to the Logos of God to seek the Rhema of God. The Logos is what God said. The Rhema is what God is saying to you today.

# CHAPTER 4

# THE BIBLE AND DAILY DYNAMIC ENCOUNTERS WITH GOD - 3

*"O God, thou art my God, I seek thee,*
*my soul thirsts for thee; my flesh faints for thee,*
*as in a dry and weary land where no water is.*
*So I have looked upon thee in the sanctuary,*
*beholding thy power and glory.*
*Because thy steadfast love is better than life,*
*my lips will praise thee.*
*So I will bless thee as long as I live;*
*I will lift up my hands and call on thy name.*
*My soul is feasted as with marrow and fat,*
*and my mouth praises thee with joyful lips,*
*When I think of thee upon my bed,*
*and meditate on thee in the watches of the night;*
*For thou hast been my help,*
*and in the shadow of thy wings I sing for joy.*
*My soul clings to thee; thy right hand upholds me"*
(Psalm 63:1-8).

## 1. REMINDER

You are about to approach the Word of God. Make sure that you have been emptied of the following :

a)   Your previous opinion about the subject or passage.

b)   Any other prejudices you may have because of what others have taught about the passage that offended you.

c)   Any other prejudices you may have because of what others have taught about the passage that pleased you.

d)   Any burdens that you may have about your walk with God, your ministry, your family, your finances ...

e)   Any fear that God will demand from you something that you are not able to do or give. Fear blocks communion.

f)   Etc.

Unless you have emptied yourself of these things and any others that the Lord might show you, you are likely to put into the passage what God does not have in it, or to let your problem change the message of the passage. You must come open-hearted and empty-handed to the Lord; so that you may receive what He has for you. You should come expecting something new from the Lord. He has billions of new things. Expect one or more of them. Do not expect Him to deal with you as in the past. Expect surprises. The Bible says, "*What no eye has seen, nor ear heard, nor the heart of man conceived, what God has prepared for those who love him*" (1 Corinthians 2:9).


## 2. FACE THE PASSAGE

Read the passage once. Read it again. Read it a third time. As you read you may begin to receive some thoughts and ideas into your spirit and mind. It could be that one particular thought has gripped your heart or one particular command has pierced through to your heart. Note such a thought or command down. That may be the principal area in which you are going to base your meditation.

It could be that after you have read the passage three times, nothing in you is awakened. The Word seems lifeless to you. You are untouched. Do not despair. Turn to the Lord and pray something like this: "Lord, You are the Author of the passage I have read. The Words that You spoke and Your Word which You caused to be written are spirit and life. This passage is spirit and life. Cause my spirit to respond to the spirit and life in this passage. Thank You, Lord, that You have heard me and You are answering me even now.

Amen." Now, turn to the passage and read it again. You may find that your spirit wakens to something in the passage, or that you see in it something that you did not see before. If you see some such thing, that will be the thing to meditate on that day.

Should it be that after the prayer and further reading you still do not have your being respond to anything in the passage, if God has not supernaturally taken over to talk to you, you should not despair. The first time you asked. The second time you sought. Now you must knock. Cry out to the Lord. Say to Him, "My Father, I refuse this silence. You are my Father. I have a right to hear Your voice. What would I be if I did not hear Your voice? How would I face the day, Lord? You promised that You would answer me. Lord, speak to me. I have confessed all the sins in my life to You; yet I am far from perfect. If there is something in my life that displeases You, Lord, forgive me because of the death of Christ on the cross and turn now, Lord, and make your Word alive to me. Lord, I believe that You will speak to me now and I thank You for it. Amen."

After that, you will find something in the passage that comes alive to you.

Having found that on which to meditate, you want to now turn to it and concentrate on it. A number of things may have come to your heart as you were reading the Word. You may find that there are two or three or even four new thoughts or impressions. If you try to meditate on each one of them, you may find that you become superficial or that your heart will become heavy with many things. You will have written those thoughts down in your quiet time book. Now you should thank the Lord for each one of them. You should now say to the Lord, "Of these thoughts, one of them is the special message that You have for me today. Lord, show it to me." Now turn to the thoughts that you wrote down and read them over with a prayer. You will find that one of them seems to leap out of the page and arrest you and more or less possesses you. That is the one you are to meditate on.

The particular thought that has come forth may be an attribute of God the Father, the Son, or the Holy Spirit. It may be a word of encouragement. It may be a command. It may be a sin, or anything. How you will proceed with the meditation will depend on what the Father has said to you. I suggest the following, but feel free to move as the Spirit leads you. You will find that how you move will vary from day to day, and that there is no standard way to proceed. It is only important that you proceed under the leadership of the Holy Spirit.

Make a short summary, in your own words, of what the passage is saying on the particular thing that God has touched you about. If it is about a particular command to obey, then summarise what that command is saying in the context of the passage at hand. I will illustrate what I am saying from a Bible passage. 1 Thessalonians 5:23-24 says, "*May the God of peace himself sanctify you wholly; and may your spirit and soul and body be kept sound and blameless at the coming of our Lord Jesus Christ. He who calls you is faithful, and He will do it.*" Let us take for granted that the particular thing that hit you or came alive to you is the part, "He who calls you is faithful." A summary of the thought in the context of the passage could be something like the following: "The apostle desires that God sanctify all of me, that all of me be kept sound and blameless at the return of Christ. The God who has called me is faithful and that faithful God will sanctify me wholly."

This summary is necessary so that words, thoughts ... are not taken out of their Bible context and therefore made to say what the Lord never intended them to say. I consider it a wrong approach to the Word, if, after the above passage has been read, someone should decide to meditate on the word "peace". The passage is talking, not of peace, but of the God of Peace. To isolate peace would lead you to having the passage say what you want. The same thing will apply to anyone who wants to use this passage to study and meditate on the words "spirit" or "soul" or "body." All meditation must be in the context of the passage.

After a person has summarised what the passage is saying or the thought that he is meditating upon, he should do some analysis. This will further help him to understand what he is meditating upon. He could write the result of that analysis down as follows:

a)   God is the One who personally sanctifies.

b)   God sanctifies wholly.

c)   God sanctifies spirit, soul, and body.

d)   What God sanctifies can be kept sound and blameless all through life, until the Lord Jesus returns.

e)   God has called me to Himself.

f)   God has called me with the goal of sanctifying me wholly.

g)   God can be trusted to sanctify me wholly.  He will do it.

Then the person can now move on.  He can pray, "Lord, You are the One who called me. You called me to Yourself.  You also called me to sanctification."  The person can stop and pray thanking God for the double call that he has received.  He may then thank God that He has not only called him to sanctification but that He has taken upon  Himself to do the sanctification.  He may further thank the Lord that He has taken upon Himself not only to sanctify but to sanctify wholly. This may give a new hope to the one who is meditating.  He may come to a new plane of assurance that the work of sanctification in him which is apparently going very slowly, will certainly be accomplished. This thought may lead to worship and adoration and endless thanksgiving.

The person meditating may now wish to turn to the Lord to confess particular areas in his life in which he has known much defeat. The sins or the failures should be stated very clearly. No vagueness is permitted in meditation. You are before the Lord. You should at least be honest, even if it is for the first time in your life. You can now name the besetting sins in your life. You can say to Him, "Lord, I commit the sin of worrying. I committed it today and I have committed it many times. Today, I worried about this thing and the other thing. I often commit this sin of worry about the fact that I am not yet married, I do not yet have children, I am jobless, my job is threatened ...  Lord, I also commit the sin of adultery in my heart. I do not commit it in general, but I often commit it with ...... Lord, I also commit the sin of gossiping. I gossip about the people in general but I gossip particularly about the brethren. I gossip particularly about sister..... and brother ..... I gossiped about him two days ago and repented, yet, yesterday I committed the same sin of gossiping about him."

The person may want to ask the Lord to create in him a heart that hates sin, in addition to being forgiven. He may now turn to the Lord and plead with Him to deliver him from these chains since He called him to sanctification and since He who called him is faithful and able to sanctify him wholly.

Another thing he could do is to think of other areas in his life in which he was once bound by sin and bound so firmly that he thought that there might be no hope for him. However, he did turn to the Lord who called him and is faithful and He delivered him permanently. He can write down such areas and say, "I was once held in bondage in this area and You delivered me. Glory be to Your Holy name! I was also held captive in this other area and You set me permanently free. May Your name be exalted! You are the Deliverer,

O Lord. You answer prayers. To You all flesh shall come on account of sin and be set free. Glory, glory, glory be ascribed to You! Amen."

There are times when after reading the passage and finding those areas that have application to one's life and working out the application, you may feel empty and unfulfilled. You have met the Word of God. You have seen how you will apply it in your life, but you have not met the Lord. That is why you are unfulfilled.

First of all, we suggest that you should thank the Lord that you made progress in your relationship with Him to the point where you are able to distinguish between meeting His Word and its application and meeting Him. It is a mark of immaturity that someone be satisfied when they bring him a letter and a gift from his fiancée and the person is so satisfied that he no longer wants the fiancée. Mature people, indeed all mature lovers, would be glad to see the letter and the gift, but they would be unfulfilled. Only the presence of the fiancée would satisfy them at the deeper level.

So the one who has met the Word and its application but has not been touched by the Lord, must go back to the Lord. He must confess the situation as it is. He should tell the Lord, "Thank you for Your Word and its application to my life for today. However, I need You. Only You can satisfy me. Lord, reach out to me and give me Yourself. Lord, do not let me go into the day unfulfilled. Touch me and I will be fulfilled." As he continues to talk to the Lord in this way, he may be led to read that part of the passage that touched him before or the entire passage. He may be led just to continue to speak to the Lord, supplicating before His throne and pleading with Him. He may continue to plead and sob and weep before Him. It will all depend upon the depth of his longing for the Lord if he is to cry out to the Lord. Anyway, he will go as far as his hunger takes him and press on according to the desire of his heart. What will happen will vary with the person, the depth of his hunger and what the Lord in His sovereignty wants to do. I can only say that I know that the

Lord will reach out to the person and satisfy him. It may be that the Lord will call his name, and that on hearing the Lord's voice his hunger will suddenly cease. It may be that the Lord will reach out and touch him as a father touches a child, laying his hand on his head and saying to him, "Son, I love you." It may be a word from the Lord that will answer to a deep present need in him and say, "I will be with you. Do not be afraid. I am going with you into the situation. You should count on Me." It may be that on reading the passage, while pleading for the Lord's touch, he will see something of the Lord in the passage that will satisfy his hunger for the Lord and his heart will be full of rejoicing. It may be that the Lord will speak a word of rebuke to him that is direct, personal and heart-breaking, that will lead to tears and so on.  All we say is that He will do something to the waiting soul. We even say that He must do something for the hungry soul. He has made the following promises and all who come to Him can trust Him and believe Him to fulfil His Word.

"*I love those who love me, and those who seek me diligently find me*" (Proverbs 8:17).


There will be times when, after one has read the passage once or twice, the Lord takes over and begins to speak directly. I do not want to discuss the matter of the Lord talking directly here. I only know that there will be times when He will take over and talk to you about some matter that may have nothing to do with the passage which is before you. I have known such times in my daily dynamic encounters with Him. On one such occasion, He started to give me instructions about the work. As He spoke to me, I wrote down what He was saying. This lasted for two hours and what He said solved many problems that had been perplexing me then. On another occasion, He spoke directly to stop a certain relationship which was standing in His way.  On another occasion, He broke in to give me instructions about what were to be the priorities of my life.  On that particular occasion, the thing that He said was to be the number one pre-occupation of my life was the thing that I feared the most and had failed in the most. Yet He said, "Your priority work from now on shall be long fasts..." He gave eight other things that were to come after fasting. That became a turning point in my life as I had to learn to lean on Him in a way I had not yet done before, since fasting was one of my weakest points. In fact, I had thought that others were called to carry out long fasts while I was called to other areas of the ministry. But that day He spoke and reversed things, and, by His grace, they have remained reversed. Glory be to the One who calls the weak and makes them able! Indeed He delights in such things; so that no flesh may glory in His sight.

Amen.

# THE BIBLE AND DAILY DYNAMIC ENCOUNTERS WITH GOD - 4

*"O Lord, thou hast searched me and known me.*
*Thou knowest when I sit down and when I rise up;*
*thou discernest my thoughts from afar.*
*Thou searchest out my path and my lying down,*
*and art acquainted with all my ways.*
*Even before a word is on my tongue,*
*Lo, O Lord, thou knowest it altogether.*
*Thou dost beset me behind and before,*
*and layest thy hand upon me.*
*Such knowledge is too wonderful for me;*
*it is high, I cannot attain it.*
*Whither shall I go from thy Spirit?*
*Or whither shall I flee from thy presence?*
*If I ascend to heaven, thou art there!*
*If I make my bed in Sheol, thou art there!*
*If I take the wings of the morning*
*and dwell in the uttermost parts of the sea,*
*even there thy hand shall lead me,*
*and thy right hand shall hold me.*
*If I say, " Let only darkness cover me,*
*and the light about me be night,"*
*even the darkness is not dark to thee,*
*the night is bright as the day,*
*for darkness is as light with thee.*
*For thou didst form my inward parts,*
*thou didst knit me together in my mother's womb.*
*I praise thee, for thou  art fearful and wonderful.*
*Wonderful are thy works!*
*Thou knowest me right well,*
*my frame was not hidden from thee,*

*When I was being made in secret,*
*intricately wrought in the depths of the earth,*
*thy eyes beheld my unformed substance;*
*in thy book were written, every one of them,*
*the days that were formed for me,*
*when as yet there was none of them.*
*How precious to me are thy thoughts, O God!*
*How vast is the sum of them!*
*If I would count them, they are more than the*
*sand. When I awake, I am still with thee"* (Psalm 139:1-18).


## THE PLACE OF FAITH IN BIBLE MEDITATION

You came to the Word of the Lord to hear Him speak to you. He has spoken to you. You read His Word. You saw the Word (Logos) of God speak. Furthermore, you saw the Word of the Lord (Rhema) apply itself to various aspects of your life in general and to one particular area. Occasionally, the Lord spoke to you directly. We encourage you to believe that God has actually spoken to you in the above ways as the case may be. Do not allow the Enemy to sow doubt into your heart by asking you if indeed it was God who had spoken to you. Shut your heart and mind to him. At the beginning of your meditation, you asked your heavenly Father to talk to you. Could you have asked Him to talk to you and He would then allow the devil to come and talk to you to confuse you? Could you have asked for bread and He would give you a stone? Listen to the testimony of His Word: "*What father among you, if his son asks for bread, will give him a stone, or if he asks for a fish, will instead of a fish give him a serpent; or if he asks for an egg, will give him a scorpion? If you who are evil know how to give good gifts to your children, how much more will the heavenly Father give the Holy Spirit to those who ask him?*" (Luke 11:11-13).

We encourage you to believe that you have heard God's voice, that what you saw in His Word is His message to you. As you believe, you should take what you have heard seriously. You should move to the next step.

There are three main reasons why people doubt what they have received from the Lord through His Word or directly. The first one is that, too many believers believe that they are not good enough for the Lord to speak to them. They feel that they have to become some kind of super saint for the Lord to talk to them. This is very wrong. In the Bible, God spoke to ordinary believers. He even spoke to unbelievers. No one needs any special spiritual status to qualify for God to speak to him. The truth is that if anyone needs to qualify on personal merit, God may never talk to anyone, for which human being is good enough, on his own, to stand before God? We say with a clear conscience that none is qualified. Yet, He bids us listen to Him, and He speaks to us. So stop doubting and believe.

The second reason is that the offers that God makes during some times of encounters with Him are startling. One believer received a vow from God that gave him God's holiness and peace, a ministry to bless, the friendship of God and the promise that he would be made into a man full of the Holy Spirit and given a special place in God's heart in the future. The packet was so big and so far-reaching that the person began to doubt. He ought to have believed. How big our God is! Has He not promised us exceedingly great things? He says, "*Ask of me, and I will make the nations your heritage, and the ends of the earth your possession*" (Psalm 2:8). Is that not a big offer?

Does He mean it? Can He do it? He says again, "*Truly, truly I say to you, he who believes in me will also do the works that I do; and greater works than these will he do, because I go to the Father*" (John 14:12). Does He mean it? Does He really mean that He intends the one who believes in Him to do the works that He did and greater works? If He means it, then there is no limit to what the believers can do and no limit to what He can give to the believer. In fact, we need some God-sized people to receive some God-sized projects from God, receive some God-sized ability from Him and accomplish these projects; so that the current trends of an impotent and defeated Christianity may be changed to the victorious Christian faith that the Bible has promised. You should not doubt because you have received from God what you think is too big for you.

The third reason why people doubt what they have received from the Lord is that He may have spoken against a cherished sin or a cherished relationship, demanding its immediate termination. Those who prefer to keep their sin will prefer to doubt that they have heard His voice. This is sheer foolishness. I know from hard-earned experience that it is foolish to rationalise when the finger of God has pointed to a particular sin. He will keep pointing at it. You may change the book of the Bible in which you are meditating in order to run away from what God is saying, but He will pursue you all over. You may go to Genesis. His finger will point to your sin in any chapter of Genesis. You may run to Malachi, Jude or Revelation, but you will meet Him there talking about the same issue. You may decide not to meditate, but if you go somewhere, you will hear the brethren talking about that sin and its consequences. Even in your dreams, He will talk to you about it. He will continue to talk to you about it until you repent and forsake it, or until He finds that you have hardened your heart, in which case, He will give you up. We are dealing with an inescapable God. The Psalmist was well aware of this and confessed, "*Whither shall I go from thy Spirit? Or whither shall I flee from thy presence? If I ascend to heaven thou art there! If I make my bed in Sheol thou art there!*" (Psalm 139:7-8).

The best thing to do is to forsake the sin. Believe that God has actually spoken to you about it for your good, and part with it for ever. That is the pathway of wisdom! That is the pathway of blessing!!

## RECORDING WHAT HAS BEEN RECEIVED

You will no doubt have recorded all that God has spoken to you about: the revelation about Himself, the Son, and the Holy Spirit, the sins in your life, things to do in your family, your place of work or ministry, the new covenants that He has entered into with you, and so on and so forth. We repeat that it is great folly to refuse to record these things. Not to record them is a way of saying to the Enemy, "I do not want to keep these things. I want to forget them. If I record them, then I will have to obey them. As I do not want to obey them, I will just expose them and, please, come and steal them." He will snatch them away. The seed that was sown on the roadside was not covered. It was exposed. Birds hid it in their stomachs! Be wise. Some think it spiritual not to record what God has said. The Lord will soon be here and everyone shall receive his reward. We shall soon see if those who received from the Lord and forgot what they received and, therefore, did not remember to act upon it, will receive more recommendations than those who recorded all that the Lord said to them and then laboured to obey each one of them!

## WORKING OUT THE PRACTICALIMPLICATIONS OF WHAT HAS BEEN RECEIVED

God does not speak just to fill His children with intellectual knowledge. He speaks to lead His own to obedience.

God demands obedience. He has one fundamental problem with man, and that problem is that man does not obey Him. He had the problem with:-

Adam,

Cain,

The children of Israel,

Jonah,

Saul,

Solomon,

and so on.


Those who made progress with God like:-

Abraham,

Isaac,

Jacob,

Joseph,

and so on,

all made progress because they obeyed Him. People like the rich young ruler, the crowds that followed Him, the Pharisees... all had problems with the Lord Jesus because they would not obey Him.

When a person hears the voice of the Lord, regardless of how that voice has come to him, he has reached a crossroads for better or for worse. If he obeys the Lord, he is blessed. If he disobeys, he is ruined. There are  three possibilities opened to anyone after he has heard God's voice during his encounter with Him:


Disobedience

Partial obedience

Total obedience.


Those who disobey have decided that they want to overthrow God from the throne and place themselves there. They believe that they know better than God. They, in a sense, want to commit Deicide. They want to murder God; for disobedience is an attempt to murder God. Unfortunately, God cannot be murdered. Such instead commit suicide. Those who obey partially, or who decide to obey gradually, or who postpone obedience, are the same as the disobedient. They may even be worse; for they want to give the impression that they have obeyed, whereas their hearts are hardened against God. Partial obedience is worse than complete disobedience. It is disobedience plus self-deception. It is a determined effort to murder God slowly and with ruse. Unfortunately, it is also a protracted plan of suicide. Saul decided to obey God partially. It cost him all that it would have cost a disobedient king. Any reasons given for not obeying completely or for not obeying at once, are acts of self-deception. The heart of man is bare before God. None should try to deceive Him. He cannot be deceived. Promises to obey that do not lead to action are evil speech before Him. Promises of love for Him from disobedient hearts is like spitting on His face. Do not do it.

You have heard His voice. Go and obey. Go and obey at once. Go and obey completely. It may cost you everything to obey. Go ahead and obey at all cost. It may be that the matter seems to you to be a small one, like being told to go and confess a lie that you told to the one to whom you lied. God wants it done at once. It is not a small matter with God. There are no small matters with God and there are no big issues. All issues are important to Him and for all of them He demands obedience. When Saul spared the Amalekite king and some of the animals, God told him that rebellion was as the sin of divination and that stubbornness was an iniquity as serious as idolatry. God said that the partial obedience of Saul was equivalent to a total rejection of Him. He in turn rejected him from being king. In fact, Saul first disobeyed in small matters and, later on, he committed the sin of divination. Those who disobey in small matters will eventually commit other sins which are more grave.

So, decide that you will obey God at once. You promised at the beginning that you would obey Him. You vowed to Him. Keep your vow.

Part of the time for meditation should be used to work out the way in which the obedience is going to be carried out. If the Lord has told you to give some money to someone, you should decide how you are going to have the money and when you will actually hand the money to the person. If you have to write a letter of encouragement, you should fix a time on your programme that day for writing it.

Another reason why you should obey that day is that God will give you some more instructions in your quiet time of the subsequent days. If you have not carried out the commands of the day, you may be overloaded with things to do and the Enemy will begin to work on you. The other reason is that by not obeying, you reduce your opportunities of having God speak to you.

I normally write the things that I must do at the bottom of the page in my notebook in capital letters. Sometimes, I write them at the margin and encircle them so that they will catch my attention at once. I suggest that it may even be better to keep a small notebook that contains only the things that God has said to us and which we must obey.

## WHAT TO DO WITH THE THINGS RECEIVED

The riches received from the Lord can be divided into three classes. There are:

a)   Riches to keep for yourself.
b)   Riches to share with others.
c)   Riches to memorise.

## a) Riches to keep for yourself

The Lord will say some things to you that will not be expedient for you to share. He may do a new work in your heart. He may give you a new revelation. He may promote you... These things constitute your history with God. They are your milestones with Him. Keep quiet about them. Let people see the impact of what God has done in your life instead of hearing you say that God has promised you this and that and the other. You should also bear in mind that the reason you are sharing the things could be to draw attention to yourself and exalt yourself before the people of God. Self-exaltation is an abomination before God. It is pride, and the proud must be brought down by the Lord. Do not make yourself become one whom God must oppose even though He has blessed you. All believers should follow the example of Paul in this matter. He said, "*I know a man in Christ, who fourteen years ago, was caught up to the third heaven - whether in the body or out of the body I don't know, God knows. And I know that this man was caught up into Paradise - whether in the body or out of the body I do not know, God knows - and he heard things that cannot be told, which man may not utter. On behalf of this man I will boast, but on my own behalf I will not boast, except of my weaknesses*" (2 Corinthians 12:2-5). He kept quiet for fourteen years and even when he spoke he did not say the things that he had heard. They were things that could not be told, that man may not utter! May we, too, meet God, be carried into the third heaven and hear things that we cannot tell. May these things increase our love for the Lord and our commitment against His enemy and, in that way, may we build roots for the days ahead!

## b) Riches to share

There will be things received from the Lord which should be shared with those who are close to us and, maybe, with the whole assembly. That is for us to decide. The question may be asked as to how someone will know what to keep for himself and what to share. We say that the Lord will guide you. However, there is a rule that is generally helpful. It is this: Anything that you receive from the Lord that will make you look important to those who might hear you share it, should be kept between you and the Lord. Anything that will make you look small before those who will hear you - like your sins, failures or weaknesses being exposed in detail by the Lord, should be shared. It will help others more than sharing your great-ness. The apostle Paul said that he was going to boast of his weak-nesses. That is good ground for boasting.

### c) Riches to memorise.

There will be verses, part of a verse or some word that come from the Lord to you during the time of meditation, which you should memorize. The Lord might have said to you, "Fear not. I am going into this battle with you." Memorise that and repeat it during the day, and more so during the battle. He might also say to you, "No liar shall enter the kingdom of God." Memorize that, so that it will help you to be alert. You may want to write what you have memo-rized somewhere so that you may see it very often. Do so.

## THE EXPANDING NATURE OF SOME MEDITATIONS

There will be some meditations during which the Lord will say something to you that needs to become the subject of another me-ditation. Do not resist this and move on to a new passage. If, for example, you are meditating on husbands loving their wives and you find that it is necessary to seek God's face as to whether or not you should save some money for your wife and children in case of any eventualities, you may feel that you want to meditate and hear what

God will say to you about the issue, since you are not to keep treasures on earth but to transfer them at once to heaven as Jesus taught. You may then set the next day to meditate on this issue, examining your heart before God and allowing Him to examine it while you seek His voice and listen to His voice. You may even find that the matter is not settled in two meditations and that a third and maybe a fourth and even a fifth one may be necessary. Pray about it and move as God leads you.

## DYNAMIC ENCOUNTERS WITH CHRIST AND BEARING THE MARK OF THE GLORY OF GOD

If God has spoken to you, if you have really encountered Him, He will leave a mark on you which will abide throughout the day. You will be different. No one ever met God and was the same. If you obey Him, you will carry a joy and a radiance with you that is obvious for all to see. You will be more loving. You will be at peace. You will be gracious. You will have a clear sense of direction for the day and a clearer sense of direction for life. If, on the other hand, you decide to disobey, you will be more miserable. Normally, those who sincerely seek God on a daily basis are all students in the School of Obedience. They hear His voice. They obey Him and they are changed.

Glory be to His name!

# CHAPTER 6

# PRAYER AND DAILY DYNAMIC ENCOUNTERS WITH GOD - 1

*"The Lord answer you in the day of trouble!*
*The name of the God of Jacob protect you!*
*May he send you help from the sanctuary,*
*and give you support from Zion!*
*May he remember all your offerings,*
*and regard with favour your burnt sacrifices!*
*May he grant you your heart's desire,*
*and fulfil all your plans!*
*May we shout for joy over your victory,*
*and in the name of our God set up our banners!*
*May the Lord fulfil all your petitions!*
*Now I know that the Lord will help his anointed;*
*He will answer him from his holy heaven*
*with mighty victories by his right hand*
*some boast of chariots, and some of horses;*
*but we boast of the name of the Lord our God.*
*They will collapse and fall;*
*but we shall rise and stand upright"*  (Psalm 20:1-7).

## 1. GOD'S CALL TO PRAY

God has called men to prayer. He has ordained prayer as the mechanism through which redeemed people will share His sovereignty with Him. The praying saint can move God who can move the universe in any direction. This means that the praying saint can determine all that happens in the universe.

Below are some of God's calls to prayer drawn from His Word.

1.  *"Call upon me in the day of trouble; I will deliver you, and you shall glorify me"* (Psalm 50:15).

2.  *"Pray therefore the Lord of the harvest to send out labourers into his harvest"* (Matthew 9:38).

3.  *"Ask and it will be given you, seek, and you will find; knock, and it will be opened to you"* (Matthew 7:7).

4.  *"Whatever you ask in my name, I will do it, that the Father may be glorified in the Son. If you ask anything in my name, I will do it"* (John 14:13-14).

5.  *"Hitherto you have asked nothing in my name, ask and you will receive, that your joy may be full"* (John 16:24).

You have been called to prayer.


## 2. GOD'S PROMISE TO ANSWER PRAYER

God has not only promised to answer prayers. He has promised to answer prayers in a limitless way. He has put His whole integrity into the matter. If He failed to answer prayers, He would be failing to be Himself. He says in his Word,

1.  *"Truly I say to you, if you ask anything of the Father he will give it to you in my name"* (John 16:23).

2.  *"For every one who asks receives and he who seeks finds, and to him who knocks it will be opened"* (Luke 11:10).

3.  *"Ask of me and I will make the nations your heritage, and the ends of the earth your possession"* (Psalm 2:8).

## 3. BIBLE MEN PRAYED AND GOD ANSWERED

The men of the Bible prayed. The following are a few examples

1.  Abraham prayed for a son and God gave him Isaac.
2.  Abraham prayed for Ishmael and God heard him.
3.  Isaac prayed to the Lord for his wife Rebecca because she was barren and the Lord granted his prayer and she conceived and bore Esau and Jacob.
4.  Jacob prayed for deliverance from Esau and God delivered him.
5.  Moses cried to the Lord for water for the children of Israel and God answered him.
6.  Moses prayed that God might not disinherit Israel and God heard him.
7.  Moses prayed that the Lord might show him His glory and God did so.
8.  Moses prayed that he might be allowed into the land of Canaan and he was. (He was on the mountain with the Lord at the transfiguration, his prayer having been answered 1500 years later).
9.  Joshua prayed because Israel lost the first battle with Ai and God heard him.
10. Gideon prayed asking for a sign of victory and God gave him.
11. Hannah prayed for a son and God gave her three sons and two daughters.
12. Etc.

## 4.  DAVID'S WHOLE LIFE WAS GIVEN TO PRAYER

In one psalm after another, he prayed. The entire Psalm 3 is a prayer. "O Lord, how many are my foes! Many are rising against me..." Psalm 4 begins with a prayer. All of Psalms 5, 6, 7, 8, 9... are prayers. Some are praises. Some are thanksgiving, some are cries for protection, some are cries of repentance, some are the deep longings for the heart of God...

All of David's life, as exemplified by the Psalms, was given to prayer. He was a man of much meditation. He was a man of much prayer. He was also a man who was heard by God in an exemplary way.

There is no one who prayed and God refused to answer him. God has always honoured His commitment to answer prayer. He will never withdraw that commitment.

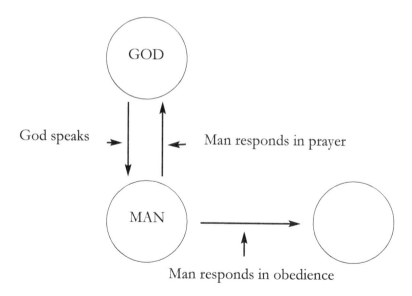

*The inten relationship between GOD Speaking and man responding*

## PRAYER AND THE THINGS REVEALED

As we have already seen, God will speak during your time of meditation. You will respond to Him by prayer and by obedience. It is not necessary to say that you will meditate and afterwards pray. There is a sense in which this is not true. During meditation you are praying as well as listening and hearing God's voice. You start meditation in prayer and with prayer. You continue meditation in prayer and you bring your meditation to an end by prayer. It is a dynamic process. When the Lord speaks, you respond by praise, thanksgiving or a prayer of repentance. He may again speak and you may respond by a prayer of intercession. He may show you something that the enemy is planning to do against you or someone else, and you immediately move to prayer to demolish his plans and works.

It could be that all that you record in your meditation book on some days, are the responses in prayer to what the Lord is saying to you from His Word.

If the Lord shows you something of His glory, thank Him at once for it. Do not say that this is the time for meditation and that you will wait for the time of prayer afterwards. If you wait, you may quench the Spirit. If you are shown a sin, confess it at once and clear the way for God to speak on.

It is because we should respond in prayer as we go along in the meditation that we call it dynamic encounters with God. It is because we start with prayer and then the Word and then prayer and then the Word that it is indeed dynamic. We ask Him to speak and He speaks. He speaks and we respond. We read His Word and He does not speak and we pray and pray until He speaks. All of it goes hand in hand.

I, again, encourage the saints to pray as they meditate and not leave prayer as an isolated event to come after they have finished hearing God.

## THE DANGER OF MONOLOGUES

It is possible to make God have monologues with man and vice versa. If a person says that for the first hour he will listen to God speak to him and after that he will speak to God for the next one hour, he may be forcing God and himself into monologues.

If the Lord shows you something wonderful about the Lord Jesus or blesses you in a new way and you do not respond but say, "I will finish hearing His voice and then I will respond," then you are building a cold, formal and poor relationship.

If you come with your prayer topics and say, "Lord, I thank You for this and that and the other. I need the following things today: a,b,c,and d. I have the following difficulties: a, b, c, and d. I do not understand the following things that You said to me last week a, b, c, d..." you are carrying out a monologue.

Dialogue or, better, fellowship means that when God speaks, we respond. We ask questions and receive answers. We respond spontaneously. When told to carry out some acts of obedience, we thank Him for honouring us with such a charge and then ask for details that were not given, or that were given but we missed.

Dynamic encounters mean that there is continuous flow between God and the meditating saint from the beginning to the end, and that all along, both parties are speaking and listening to each other.

This is clearly illustrated in the life of Abraham. The Bible says, *"And God said to Abraham, 'As for Sarai your wife, you shall not call her name Sarai, but Sarah shall be her name. I will bless her, and moreover I will give you a son by her; I will bless her, and she shall be a mother of nations; kings of people shall come from her.' Then Abraham fell on his face and laughed, and said to himself, 'Shall a child be born to a man who is a hundred years old? Shall Sarah who is ninety years old, bear a child?' And Abraham said to God, 'O that Ishmael might live in thy sight.' God said, 'No but Sarah your wife shall bear a son, and you shall call his name Isaac. I will establish my covenant with him as an everlasting covenant for his descendants after him. As for Ishmael, I have heard you; be-*

*hold, I will bless him and make him fruitful and multiply him exceedingly; he shall be the father of twelve princes, and I will make him a great nation*" (Genesis 17:15-21).

This is dynamic encounter. God spoke. Abraham responded. God answered.

It happened with Abraham. It ought to happen today. It is happening with multitudes. It should happen with you. Let it happen with you.

God spoke to you. Respond to Him. You may respond with:-

1.  Praise,
2.  Thanksgiving,
3.  Repentance,
4.  Confession,
5.  A song or
6.  A vow.

### Responding with a song

Songs are the outflow of the heart God-wards. There is a time when a person coldly decides that he will sing a song to the Lord. He thus sings a song either from memory or from a hymn book. There is, however, a time when the song flows from the person God-wards. It just comes. He reaches a point in His fellowship with God where without any pre-thought or any effort, a song flows out to the Lord. This is glorious. Sometimes, it is a song that was learnt in the past. At other times, it is new words being spontaneously given to an old tune. On rarer occasions, it is a new tune altogether with words just flowing from the heart to God. This is wonderful. At other times, it is a song flowing forth to the Lord in words that are not known to you but to God. The Lord should be praised for these different responses in song to God. The Bible commands us to sing to the Lord.

1.   *"Sing praises to the Lord, who dwells in Zion!"* (Psalm 9:11).

2.   *"Sing praises to the Lord, O you his saints, and give thanks to his holy name"* (Psalm 30:4).

3.   *"Sing praises to God, sing praises! Sing praises to our King, sing praises!"* (Psalm 47:6).

4.   *"Sing to the Lord with thanksgiving, making melody to our God upon the lyre"* (Psalm 147:7).

In addition to the general command to sing praises to the Lord, there are definite commands in the Word that the saints should sing a new song unto the Lord. Below are some examples of the command.

1.   *"Sing to him a new song, play skilfully on the strings, with loud shouts"* (Psalm 33:3).

2.   *"Praise the Lord! Sing to the Lord a new song, his praise in the assembly of the faithful"* (Psalm 149:1).

The Psalmist committed himself to sing to the Lord. He said:

1.   *"I will give to the Lord the thanks due to his righteousness, and I will sing praise to the name of the Lord, the Most High"* (Psalm 7:17).

2.    *"I will be glad and exult in thee, I will sing praise to thy name, O Most High"* (Psalm 9:2).

3.    *"I will sing to the Lord, because he has dealt bountifully with me"* (Psalm 13:6).

4.    *"But I will rejoice for ever, I will sing praises to the God of Jacob"* (Psalm 75:9).

5.    *"I will sing a new song to thee, O God; upon a ten-stringed harp I will play to thee"* (Psalm 144:9).

Singing unto the Lord is the response of grateful hearts. It is response. As people know the Lord deeper and deeper, they flow more and more in singing to Him. They see His glory. They experience His love and mercy and they cannot but sing to Him.

Normally, when a person's walk with God is normal, most meditations will end with a spontaneous song to the Lord.

If there is no spontaneous song flowing from your heart to Him, I encourage you to take a hymn book and sing unto Him. This is good and acceptable. Sometimes, after the song from the hymn book, songs will begin to flow spontaneously from the heart unto the Lord.

Be sure to respond to the Lord in song. Be free to open your meditation with a song. Have the liberty to sing a song when you have read the passage but received nothing from the Lord. Sing a song of praise and it could be that after the song has been sung, everything will change and the passage will come alive. When you have handled the practical applications of a passage of the Word but have not the satisfying touch of God, feel free to sing a song of praise, thanking the Lord for the fact that you have not touched Him. You may find that before the song has ended, you are lost in Him. His glory has overshadowed you and you are lost in each other. In these things there are no laws and no rules. What I write here is the fruit of twenty years of Bible meditation. The songs have served different purposes at different times. I have tried to be led by the Spirit each time. Whenever I thought that I had found a formula which I could apply mechanically, I lost the sense of God's presence. I thank God that it has been so; for God wants us to be led by the Spirit and not by rules, laws and formulae. Amen.

### Responding with tears

There are songs of rejoicing. We thank God for them. Many meditations will end in rejoicing, but all meditations will not end in rejoicing. Some will end in tears. It will all depend on what the Lord has shown us or said to us. He may show us what is wrong with us that needs deep repentance. He may even show us that there are things wrong in us for which He must chasten us. He may show us that He is going to deal with us so as to humble us. He may open our eyes to see ourselves as He sees us. He may show us that He is going to have to cleanse the church through judgment, or that His wrath must surely come upon the nation. We cannot go away from hearing His voice in this way without pain and a cry to Him. The Psalmist knew such moments. During one of them, he prayed, "*O Lord, rebuke me not in thy anger, nor chasten me in thy wrath! For thy arrows have sunk into me, and thy hand has come down on me. There is no soundness in my flesh because of thy indignation; there is no health in my bones because of my sin. For my iniquities have gone over my head; they weigh like a burden too heavy for me. My wounds grow foul and fester because of my foolishness, I am utterly bowed down and prostrate, all the day I go about mourning for my loins are filled with burning and there is no soundness in my flesh. I am utterly spent and crushed; I groan because of the tumult of my heart. Lord, all my longing is known to thee, my sighing is not hidden from thee*" (Psalm 38:1-9).

I have known many such meditations over the last twenty years.

There have been times when the Lord has met me in the morning and spoken to me and I have wished that the ground would open and swallow me for shame. There have been times when my only response to Him has been tears, cries and groans. Yes, there have been times when I have felt that the best thing would be for Him to banish me from His presence for ever.

However, He did not banish me. He did not throw me away. I sang a song of mourning and repentance. I thanked Him for my dreadful sins and I begged Him to forgive me, cleanse me and restore me.

How good our God is! How wonderful His love is! How limitless His mercy is! He heard me. He cleansed me. He pardoned me. He restored me and He changed my sorrow into rejoicing and my tears into shouts of joy. That is why I can write this message this day. Glory, glory, glory to His holy name!

### Responding with a vow

You may feel led to make a vow unto the Lord, depending on how He has dealt with you. He might have shown you the full range of the finished work of Christ and you are led to vow never to live for self but to live always for Him who loved you and gave His all for you. You may want to make a vow to Him about it. Do it, but remember that if you make a vow, you will have to pay it. You may vow to give Him a certain portion of your income for the rest of your life. You may vow to obey Him in everything for the rest of your life. You may vow to respond to a particular costly call. Whatever is the case, think carefully before you vow. Do not utter vows hastily. Do not make hasty, emotional commitments to give things to the Lord about which you will regret a few minutes after. Do not decide to go on long fasts that you will dread the very thought of a few hours afterwards. Do not try to prove tough. Do not make too many suggestions to the Lord about what you want to do. Why not ask like Saul of Tarsus, "*What shall I do, Lord?*" (Acts 22:10), and wait for Him to tell you what should be done?

Having said this, we encourage you to respond whole-heartedly to the Lord. Be spontaneous in your flow to Him. Take giant steps with Him. Commit yourself to Him and to His battles. Trust Him to make you able to do that which you have committed yourself to do. Do not be too calculative. Love is not mathematical. Love gives all and gives all spontaneously.

Mary broke her alabaster box of precious ointment on Him.

Peter and the others forsook all to follow Him.

Moses forsook Egypt to follow Him and lead His people.

C.T. Studd forsook fame, wealth, a wife and all, to go and serve Him.

All these people responded on the spur of the moment and they changed history. Will you be one such? Is today the day of action for you? God bless you!

# CHAPTER 7

# PRAYER AND DAILY DYNAMIC ENCOUNTERS WITH GOD - 2

*"Upon your walls, O Jerusalem, I have set watchmen, all the day and all the night they shall never be silent. You who put the Lord in remembrance, take no rest, and give him no rest until he establishes Jerusalem and makes it a praise in the earth"* (Isaiah 62:6-7).

*"All nations surrounded me, in the name of the Lord I cut them off! They surrounded me, surrounded me on every side, in the name of the Lord I cut them off! They surrounded me like bees, they blazed like a fire of thorns; in the name of the Lord I cut them off!"* (Psalm 118:10-12).

*"For though we live in the world, we are not carrying on a worldly war, for the weapons of our warfare are not worldly but have divine power to destroy strongholds. We destroy arguments and every proud obstacle to the knowledge of God, and take every thought captive to obey Christ, being ready to punish every disobedience, when your obedience is complete"* (2 Corinthians 10:3-6).

## 1. PRAYING THE ACTIVITIES OF THE DAY THROUGH

We have written on the need to respond spontaneously to God in prayer. However, that is not the whole story. We said that this particular meditation had to be in the morning so that all the activities of the day might be sorted out before God. It is, therefore, necessary to pray through the activities of the day.

You obviously know some of the things that await you in the day:

1.   Bathing
2.   Dressing
3.   Breakfast
4.   Going to work
5.   All that will happen at work

6.  Going back home
7.  The afternoon meal
8.  Siesta
9.  Going back to work
10. All that will happen at work
11. Getting back home in the evening
12. Supper
13. The activities of the evening, (prayer, ministry to the brethren, etc.)
14. The night

You will also want to pray for:
1.  Your partner
2.  The children
3.  All who are in your household
4.  Any visitors staying with you
5.  All the financial transactions of the day
6.  The car
7.  and others.

Pray about each of these things, putting each under the blood of the Lord. Pray for any difficulties that you foresee. Leave nothing out. You may write prayer topics or just pray, but by all means pray.

## 2. WATCHING - GODWARD

After praying through the activities of the day that are known to you, you should now turn to the Lord and ask Him to show you His plans for the day that are different from your normal routine. Be quiet before Him and maintain a spirit of praise and thanksgiving. The Lord will show you things.

He may say to you that someone will come to you to ask for help and that you must give him the needed help. He may tell you that you will be facing a strenuous day and therefore you need to relax. He may show you that someone is ill in the hospital and that you need to go and visit him. He may show you the answer to a long standing problem. He may show you someone who needs to hear the gospel and to whom you need to go and render ministry. What he will show you will vary with what is going to happen. Sometimes He will show you nothing, thereby making you know that you will have a day with the normal routine.

You should now respond to the things He has shown you. You can write prayer topics about the things and pray about them, or you may want to pray spontaneously as He shows you. There is no rule. If He shows you some future event, you should write it down so as to pray until it has happened or is over.

## 3. WATCHING - SATANWARD

While waiting before the Lord, ask Him to show you any plans that Satan has made for that day against:

you,

your job,

family: wife, children and all,

your property,

your ministry,

your assembly,

all that concerns you, your friends, etc.

The Lord may show you that Satan plans to attack your marriage with a stupid quarrel. He may show you that he will be attacking you or someone you love with sickness, or that he will attack the academic work, job, health, property of your beloved friend. He may show you the devil's plan to attack your job or others in your job, or He may show you the devil's plans against your ministry:

the personnel,

the machines,

the correspondence,

and so on.

Whatever the Lord shows you that the devil wants to do should be written down. On the other hand, you may want to come against the devil in the name of the Lord Jesus and put his plans to nought. Speak directly to Satan in the name of the Lord Jesus . Rebuke him and bring his plan or plans to nought. Command him and his hosts to leave you and yours permanently. As you command him, you should destroy any strongholds that he might already have established where he intended to attack. Liberate people of the evil thoughts that he has sown in their minds. Do not spare him.

## 4. THE NEED TO ATTACK

It is important that the plans of the devil against you be brought to nought before they are executed. Do not get into defensive warfare with him. Always attack first. The reason is obvious. It is like in football. The team that wants to win the game labours to ensure that the game is played away from its goal area and, as much as possible, in the goal area of the opponent. This will ensure that the slightest mistake made by the opponents, leads to a goal against them. In the same way, if the believer attacks Satan first, Satan will suffer the casualties. Israel won in the six-day war because her planes attacked the Egyptian planes while these were still on the ground. They were thus grounded permanently. In this way Israel, who was less armed than Egypt, won the war in April 1967. Had Israel not attacked the Egyptians before Egypt attacked, the loss to her (Israel) would have been indescribable.

You have the weapons of warfare against the devil. Use them. Be aggressive. Look out for the enemy and hit him mercilessly. Remember that if you are passive or are attacking too slowly, the enemy may hit you first, giving you wounds that you could have avoided.

Learn to attack!
Attack!
Refuse to be passive!
Be aggressive!

## 5. PRAYER TOPICS

You will record two lots of prayer topics during your quiet time — Those for immediate use and those for future use. You have a limited time of prayer in the morning. You may want to pray then only for the things that are urgent and that concern the day that is immediately ahead of you. You will then want to record the other prayer topics that concern events that are not immediately applicable into your book, too, and pray for them afterwards. By recording them, you are making sure that you will remember them and do justice to them.

## 6. RESTING IN THE LORD

After you have prayed the day through and watched before the Lord and watched against the enemy, a deep sense of peace will come over you. You have prayed the day through. Things are under control. You have committed all that you have not been able to pray about to the Lord. You are at rest.

You can now face the day with assurance. Praise the Lord about it and go into the day assured of victory in the Lord and rest in Him.

Thank the Lord for your time of meditation and go your way rejoicing. Your joy will flow to others. Those who meet you will touch life, and it will be obvious that you have been with the Lord.

Glory be to His holy name! Amen.

# CHAPTER 8

# DAILY DYNAMIC ENCOUNTERS WITH GOD ALL THE DAY LONG

*"Lord, thou hast been our dwelling place in all generations. Before the mountains were brought forth, or ever thou hadst formed the earth and the world, from everlasting to everlasting thou art God"* (Psalm 90:1-2).

*"Seven times a day I praise thee for thy righteous ordinances"* (Psalm 119:164).

*"Evening and morning and at noon I utter my complaint and moan, and he will hear my voice"* (Psalm 55:17).

*"They shall see his face and his name shall be on their foreheads. And night shall be no more; they need no light of lamp or sun, for the Lord God will be their light, and they shall reign for ever and ever"* (Revelation 22:4-5).

## 1. COMMUNION

The Lord Jesus met His Father early in the morning. They had fellowship. However, they did not only have fellowship. They had communion. The dynamic encounter continued every second of the day. He continued to be in constant touch and in constant union with His Father. He never left the Father's presence. No cloud ever came between the Father and the Son for all the years of His earthly pilgrimage, except during those hours on the cross when He bore our sins, and the Father was obliged, by His holiness, to turn His face away from Him. So, at all the other times, there was union and communion. They were not separated because He was healing or preaching or doing carpentry. His spirit and the Father's Spirit remained in vital union and communion. This is communion.

Communion is the constant, continuous and inseparable union of two spirits.

## 2. THE LORD CALLS US TO WORSHIP

It is good to come into God's presence in the morning for fellowship with Him. We thank God for that. However, God desires something more from us. He desires that we worship Him in spirit and in truth. He said, *"But the hour is coming, and now is when the true worshippers will worship the Father in spirit and truth, for such the Father seeks to worship him. God is spirit, and those who worship him must worship in spirit and truth"* (John 4:23-24). It is possible to worship the Lord in spirit and truth all the time. It is possible for the believer who has been totally delivered from all lying and all falsehood to have his spirit in vital communion with God twenty-four hours each day. It means living actively in the immediate presence of God. The Psalmist said, *"Lord, thou hast been our dwelling place in all generations"* (Psalm 90:1). It is possible to have God as the dwelling place from which one never departs. It is said of Anna that, *"She did not depart from the temple, worshipping with fasting and prayer night and day"* (Luke 2:37). In the Kingdom to come, those who will be counted worthy to attain unto it will have constant union and constant communion with the Lord for all the billions of years. The fact that Anna never departed from the physical temple for over fifty years must suggest that it is possible to live in vital communion with the Lord for the same length of time and more, having the human spirit, which is the temple of the Holy Spirit, in vital communion with Him. The fact that it will happen in the millennium and throughout eternity, means that some can attain unto it now. Such can begin to have and to enjoy a foretaste of the glory that is to come.

We will not develop this theme any more. We leave it to the more mature, those who have entered into the sanctified life in practical experience, and who love the Lord whole-heartedly and yearn only for Him, to think about it and pray about it.

We will continue the message at the level of all believers, that is, at the level that is attainable by all who are saved by grace.

## MORNING MEDITATION IS NOT ALL

It is wonderful to have met God in the morning and had fellowship with Him. It cannot be then that one says, "Lord, we have settled things with each other. I am now free to go. Goodbye, until tomorrow morning." This would reflect a legal relationship. True lovers do not do that. They are always looking for opportunities to meet and to share. If they part and a telephone is available, they will soon be on the phone, the one who went away from the other, reporting on his arrival. It will not be a simple, "I have arrived safely." A conversation will ensue. They will confess how wonderful the time together was, how painful the parting was and they will confess any failures in conduct during the time when they were together. They will write letters. They will send gifts. They will remain in touch.

Those who love the Lord will remain in touch with Him throughout the day. They will express their love for Him. They will sing. They will praise and they will give thanks. They will ask for guidance. They will confess any sins that they have committed since they last met. They will seek instructions on any events that were not foreseen but have happened.

## THE PSALMIST EXCELLED IN THIS

He sought the Lord in the morning. He sought Him throughout the day. The meditation of the morning only served to create appetite for more. He said:

1.  *"I bless the Lord who gives me counsel; in the night also my heart instructs me"* (Psalm 16:7).

2.  *"I remember thy name in the night, O Lord, and keep thy law"* (Psalm 119:55).

3.  *"It is good to give thanks to the Lord, to sing praises to thy name, O Most High; to declare thy steadfast love in the morning, and thy faithfulness by night"* (Psalm 92:1-2).

4.  *"At midnight I rise to praise thee, because of thy righteous ordinances"* (Psalm 119:62).

5.  *"Evening and morning and at noon I utter my complaint and moan, and He will hear my voice"* (Psalm 55:17).

6.  *"I will bless the Lord at all times; his praise shall continually be in my mouth"* (Psalm 34:1).

7.  *"Seven times a day I praise thee for thy righteous ordinances"* (Psalm 119:164).

8.  *"My eyes are awake before the watches of the night, that I may meditate upon thy promise"* (Psalm 119:148).

9.  *"When I think of thee upon my bed, and meditate on thee in the watches of the night"* (Psalm 63:6).

He also encourages us, saying, *"Be angry, but sin not; commune with your own hearts on your beds, and be silent"* (Psalm 4:4).

So in a sense, every time, every circumstance, every posture is good enough for fresh contact with the Lord. The apostle Paul exhorts the saints, saying, *"Always and for everything giving thanks in the name of our Lord Jesus Christ to God the Father"* (Ephesians 5:20).

*"Give thanks in all circumstances; for this is the will of God in Christ Jesus for you"* (1 Thessalonians 5:18).

## THE EIGHT WATCHES

Believers in Bible times had eight watches which they kept and during which they fellowshipped with their Lord. It was a matter, both of love for the Lord and discipline of the body. These two cannot be separated. The Bible talks of these watches in the following passages:

1.  *"Now Peter and John were going up to the temple at the hour of prayer; the ninth hour"* (Acts 3:1).

2.  *"About the ninth hour of the day he saw clearly in a vision an angel of God coming in and saying to him, "Cornelius"* (Acts 10:3).

3.  *"And Cornelius said, 'Four days ago, about this hour, I was keeping the ninth hour of prayer in my house; and behold, a man stood before me in bright apparel"* (Acts 10:30).

4.  *"The next day as they were on their journey and coming near the city, Peter went up on the house-top to pray, about the sixth hour"* (Acts 10:9).

5.  *"And in the fourth watch of the night he came to them, walking on the sea"* (Matthew 14:25).

6.  *"When I think of thee upon my bed, and meditate on thee in the watches of the night"* (Psalm 63:6).

The eight watches were as follows:

Day Watches:

09.00 first watch, corresponding to the Jewish third hour
12.00 second watch, corresponding to the Jewish sixth hour
15.00 third watch, corresponding to the Jewish ninth hour
18.00 fourth watch, corresponding to the Jewish twelfth hour

Night watches:

21.00 first watch
24.00 second watch
03.00 third watch
06.00 fourth watch

Peter was feeling hungry about mid-day, the sixth hour.

The Lord approached the disciples, walking on the sea, at the fourth watch of the night, which was around six o'clock in the morning.

These people set fixed times around the clock to meet God. They were disciplined. They put God first. When the Psalmist said that he praised the Lord seven times a day for His righteous ordinances, he was possibly saying that he praised God regularly at seven of the eight watches. Since he also was before the Lord at midnight, we can infer that he praised the Lord at

06.00
09.00
12.00

15.00

18.00

21.00

24.00

We can also infer that he possibly went to bed after midnight and woke up before 6.00 am. He, therefore, kept all the watches except the third watch of the night during which he was asleep.

Are we surprised that he went so far in knowing and loving the Lord?

Do we see the price that he paid?

Do we see the need for discipline?

Do we see the need for planned times of meeting God that are kept throughout life?

Must we continue to hide our indiscipline under the cover of being led by the Holy Spirit?

Were the Psalmist, the apostles, Daniel (Daniel 6:10) who set or maintained fixed times of meeting God in addition to unfixed times, led by the flesh? Are we wiser than they were? Do we know how to walk in the Spirit more than they did?

I challenge you to discipline. I challenge you to follow the example of the Psalmist and keep seven of the eight watches. I challenge you to begin perhaps to have three meetings with God a day as Daniel did. The Bible says, "*When Daniel knew that the documents had been signed, he went to his house where he had windows in his chamber opened towards Jerusalem, and he got down upon his knees three times a day and prayed and gave thanks before his God, as he had done previously*," (Daniel 6:10). He was in control because he had established the godly routine of praying and giving thanks three times everyday.

It is important to build good habits and keep to them. Let us not pretend that we are not governed by routine, by habits, by customs. All of us are. There are no exceptions. The question is whether the customs, routine or habits that govern our lives are those that are bringing us nearer to the Lord and helping us to know Him more intimately or not.

Where are those who have set aside one night a week for meeting God and wrestling in prayer? Where are those who will go on a fifteen minute retreat, four times every day?

Destroy indiscipline in your life.

Act at once.

Be disciplined.

Be a disciple, i.e. someone who is subjecting himself to discipline.

Keep your appointment with God even if the planets are not keeping their normal positions and want to fall on you.

The apostle Paul said, "*Do you not know that in a race all the runners compete, but only one receives the price? So run that you may obtain it. Every athlete exercises self-control in all things. They do so to receive a perishable wreath, but we an imperishable. Well, I do not run aimlessly, I do not box as one beating the air, but I pommel my body and subdue it lest after preaching to others I myself should be disqualified*" (1 Corinthians 9:24-27).

May you, too, exercise self-control in all things.

May you, too, pommel your body and subdue it.

May you do all that God has asked you to do.

May you meet Him at your appointed time and at all other times.

## THE NEED FOR CONTINUOUS REPENTANCE

As you go through today, if you sin, repent at once, confess your sin to the Lord and receive His cleansing. Ask and be filled with the Holy Spirit immediately you have confessed and forsaken your sin. Do not wait for the time of meeting God to put things right with Him. Do not go about doing anything without being filled with the Holy Spirit. Make being filled with the Holy Spirit one of the happy routines of your life, and you will indeed be blessed.

## THIS COULD BE YOUR LAST DAY ON EARTH

This could be your last day on earth. Make sure that there is no cloud between you and the Lord. Clear up everything; so that if indeed it turns out to be the last day, you will not be ashamed to meet Him.

In addition, never sleep with an unsettled misunderstanding between you and your:

wife,

children,

friend,

friends or

anyone.

You may wake up in eternity and you do not want to leave unsettled things behind you. They may wake up in eternity and you will be miserable that you parted so badly.

Do not leave your house in the morning, afternoon or evening or night with an unsettled matter between you and your wife or children or between you and a loved one or between you and anyone. It is better to wait, settle things and be late, than to go out with a cloud between you. It is better to break an appointment and put things right than rush to it with things broken. What if you were suddenly called home?

Even if you were not called home, is God glorified by the broken relationship? Is that exercising self-control in all things? Is your fellowship with God not broken or marred by the broken relationship between you and that person? Please, put it right.

This could be your last day on earth, so do not hold back any good thing that you can do to anyone. If you are able to show love, show it. Give yourself away completely. Give all of yourself away. You may never meet the person again and even if you ever met him, things might not be quite the same. So act now.

Someone wrote, "I shall pass this way but once. Therefore, if there is any good thing that I can do to any of my fellow human beings, let me do it now. Let me not neglect it or postpone it; for I shall not pass this way again."

May we take that counsel and act upon it and we shall not regret it.


## ETERNALLY WITH GOD

Soon the Lord will come and take us to Himself and take us to His home. We shall see Him. We shall be lost in Him and we shall rejoice that we started our fellowship with Him on earth, and how blessed we shall be!

Amen.

Ngaoundere, 5th June 1987.

# Very important

If you have not yet received Jesus as your Lord and Saviour, I encourage you to receive Him. Here are some steps to help you,

ADMIT that you are a sinner by nature and by practice and that on your own you are without hope. Tell God you have personally sinned against Him in your thoughts, words and deeds. Confess your sins to Him, one after another in a sincere prayer. Do not leave out any sins that you can remember. Truly turn from your sinful ways and abandon them. If you stole, steal no more. If you have been committing adultery or fornication, stop it. God will not forgive you if you have no desire to stop sinning in all areas of your life, but if you are sincere, He will give you the power to stop sinning.

BELIEVE that Jesus Christ, who is God's Son, is the only Way, the only Truth and the only Life. Jesus said, "*I am the way, the truth and the life; no one comes to the Father, but by me*" (John 14:6). The Bible says, "*For there is one God, and there is one mediator between God and men, the man Christ Jesus, who gave himself as a ransom for all*" (1 Timothy 2:5-6). "*And there is salvation in no one else (apart from Jesus), for there is no other name under heaven given among men by which we must be saved*" (Acts 4:12). "*But to all who received him, who believed in his name, he gave power to become children of God...*" (John 1:12). BUT,

CONSIDER the cost of following Him. Jesus said that all who follow Him must deny themselves, and this includes selfish financial, social and other interests. He also wants His followers to take up their crosses and follow Him. Are you prepared to abandon your own interests daily for those of Christ? Are you prepared to be led in a new direction by Him? Are you prepared to suffer for Him and die for Him if need be? Jesus will have nothing to do with half-hearted people. His demands are total. He will only receive and forgive those who are prepared to follow Him AT ANY COST. Think about it and count the cost. If you are prepared to follow Him, come what may, then there is something to do.

INVITE Jesus to come into your heart and life. He says, "*Behold I stand at the door and knock. If anyone hears my voice and opens the door (to his heart and life), I will come in to him and eat with him, and he with me* " (Revelation 3:20). Why don't you pray a prayer like the following one or one of your own construction as the Holy Spirit leads ?

"Lord Jesus, I am a wretched, lost sinner who has sinned in thought, word and deed. Forgive all my sins and cleanse me. Receive me, Saviour and transform me into a child of God. Come into my heart now and give me eternal life right now. I will follow you at all costs, trusting the Holy Spirit to give me all the power I need."

When you pray this prayer sincerely, Jesus answers at once and justifies you before God and makes you His child.

Please write to me and I will pray for you and help you as you go on with Jesus Christ...

If you have received the Lord Jesus-Christ after reading this book, please write to us at the following addresse :

For Europe :

Editions du Livre Chrétien

4, Rue du Révérend Père Cloarec

92400 Courbevoie

Courriel : editionlivrechretien@gmail.com

Imprimé en France par CPI
en septembre 2019

Dépôt légal : septembre 2019
N° d'impression : 154126